MATT AND TO

ULTIMATE
FOOTBALL HEROES

ROAD $^{TO}_{THE}$ EUROS

FROM THE PLAYGROUND
TO THE PITCH

DINO

First published by Dino Books in 2024,
an imprint of Bonnier Books UK,
4th Floor, Victoria House, Bloomsbury Square, London WC1B 4DA
Owned by Bonnier Books,
Sveavägen 56, Stockholm, Sweden

X @UFHbooks
X @footieheroesbks
www.heroesfootball.com
www.bonnierbooks.co.uk

Text © Matt Oldfield 2024

The right of Matt Oldfield to be identified as the author of this work has been
asserted by him in accordance with the Copyright, Designs and Patents Act 1988.

Paperback ISBN: 978 1 78946 789 5
E-book ISBN: 978 1 78946 796 3

British Library cataloguing-in-publication data:
A catalogue record for this book is available from the British Library.

Printed and bound in Great Britain by Clays Ltd, Elcograf S.p.A.

3 5 7 9 10 8 6 4 2

ULTIMATE FOOTBALL HEROES

Matt Oldfield is a children's author focusing on the wonderful world of football. His other books include **Unbelievable Football** (winner of the 2020 Children's Sports Book of the Year) and the **Johnny Ball: Football Genius** series. In association with his writing, Matt also delivers writing workshops in schools.

Cover illustration by Dan Leydon.
To learn more about Dan visit danleydon.com
To purchase his artwork visit etsy.com/shop/footynews
Or just follow him on X: @danleydon

TABLE OF CONTENTS

ACKNOWLEDGEMENTS

First of all I'd like to thank everyone at Bonnier Books for supporting me and for running the ever-expanding UFH ship so smoothly. Writing stories for the next generation of football fans is both an honour and a pleasure. Thanks also to my agent, Nick Walters, for helping to keep my dream job going, year after year.

Next up, an extra big cheer for all the teachers, booksellers and librarians who have championed these books, and, of course, for the readers. The success of this series is truly down to you.

Okay, onto friends and family. I wouldn't be writing this series if it wasn't for my brother Tom. I owe him so much and I'm very grateful for his belief in me as an author. I'm also very grateful to the rest of my family, especially Mel, Noah, Nico, and of course Mum and Dad. To my parents, I owe my biggest passions: football and books. They're a real inspiration for everything I do.

JUDE
BELLINGHAM

PART 1

WORLD CUP WONDERKID

10 November 2022

'One of my biggest dreams growing up was to play at a World Cup,' Jude posted on social media just after England announced their squad for the upcoming tournament in Qatar. 'I'm so grateful to have been given the chance to do so. Will give everything to try and make it a tournament that the country can be proud of. Let's go.'

Being a part of England's delayed Euro 2020 adventure (postponed to summer 2021 due to the global pandemic) had been an amazing experience for Jude, even if he hadn't got to play as much as he'd hoped. Now, in late 2022, still not yet twenty, heading into his second major international tournament, he was older, wiser, and waaaay better. He felt ready to step up for his country and be their main man in the middle.

But would England manager Gareth Southgate agree? For the squad's opening World Cup match against Iran, he went for a midfield three of:

Declan Rice, Mason Mount... and Jude – Yesssssssss!

On his World Cup debut, Jude took a little while to settle into the game, but once he did, he made a massive difference for England with his excellent runs from midfield. As Luke Shaw curled in a cross from the left, Jude sprinted towards the six-yard box to meet it. Then calmly and cleverly, he guided his header into the corner of the net. 1–0!

Goooooooooooooooooooaaaaaaaaaaaaaaaallllllllllllll llllllllllll!!!!!!!!!!!!!!!!!!!!

England were winning and Jude was their hero! As the crowd roared, he leapt high into the air, raising his right fist towards the sky. What a time to score his first senior international goal – on his World Cup debut!

And Jude didn't stop there. Just before half-time, he dribbled forward from the halfway line, and passed the ball to Harry Kane, who crossed it to Raheem Sterling. 3–0!

At the final whistle, the England players celebrated an impressive 6–2 victory. While it was Bukayo who collected the Player of the Match award, Jude must have been a very close second after his great goal and two key passes. Everyone was very excited about England's new midfield maestro, but Jude wasn't getting carried away.

'Start as we mean to go on,' he tweeted afterwards. 'Let's keep pushing!'

Their next match against the USA, however, turned out to be a very different kind of game. England struggled to find a way through, and so, instead of attacking, Jude spent most of his seventy minutes on the pitch defending. Oh well – although a 0–0 draw was a bit disappointing, there was no need to panic. And with a 3–0 win over Wales, England still made it through to the knockout rounds.

Next up, in the Round of 16: England faced Senegal. For the first thirty minutes, the African Champions were the better side, but eventually, England got back into the game, thanks to their new and improved midfield three. With Jordan Henderson playing in the middle alongside Declan, the team now looked more balanced, and Jude had more freedom to push forward and join the attack at every opportunity...

As soon as Harry got the ball near the halfway line, ZOOM! Jude was off, racing into the space behind the Senegal defence. When the pass arrived, he had three defenders chasing back behind him, and one defender in front of him, but Jude didn't panic. He dribbled on into the box, looking for support, and then at the crucial moment, just when it looked like his chance might have disappeared, he slipped a sublime pass between two defenders, and across to Jordan. 1–0!

'Come onnnnnn!' Jordan cried out, pointing at Jude, before running straight towards him. After going head-to-head for an intense moment, they hugged each other with passion. What an important goal they had just scored together!

And just before half-time, Jude helped England to score another. Rushing in to win the ball back just outside his own penalty area, he dribbled forward, battling his way past one defender. Now what? Looking up, Jude passed the ball left to Phil Foden, who passed it to Harry on the right. He was one on one with the keeper – surely he had to score? Yes. 2–0!

Jude had certainly achieved his aim of becoming England's main man in midfield. Another game, another two key passes, another amazing and all-action performance – what a wonderful World Cup he was having! And hopefully, there would be lots more match-winning moments to come, starting with their quarter-final against tournament favourites France.

'Bring it on!' Jude thought to himself as the teams walked out onto the pitch for kick-off. He had always been a confident kid, but now after his star performances against Iran and Senegal, he felt like he could win any battle and any match for his country.

Beating the World Champions, however, was going

to be England's toughest task yet. After an even start, France scored first in the seventeenth minute from a quick counterattack. Although Jude raced all the way back to his own box to defend, he couldn't quite block Aurélien Tchouaméni from blasting a stunning shot into the bottom corner. 1–0!

But despite that early setback, the England players didn't let their heads drop. Instead, they pushed forward positively, looking for an equaliser.

As usual, Jude was working hard at both ends of the pitch. One minute, he was back helping Kyle Walker to stop Kylian Mbappé, and the next he was forward in the France box, calling for the cross. Harry, though, decided to go for goal instead. His long-range strike dipped and swerved, but it didn't beat Lloris.

Unlucky, keep going!

Early in the second half, England finally got the goal that they deserved. As Bukayo dribbled up the right wing, Jude made another bursting run from midfield. 'Yessss!' When the ball came to him in the box, Jude could sense a defender behind him closing in, so he cleverly flicked it back to Bukayo for the one-two.

Bukayo tried to create enough space for a shot, but he was fouled by Tchouaméni.

'Penalty!' the England players cried out, and the referee said yes.

'Come onnnnnnnn!' Jude roared, pumping his fists at the fans, and his celebrations were even louder a minute later when Harry scored from the spot. 1–1!

Game on! The next goal was going to be key, but who would score it? Unfortunately for England, the next goalscorer turned out to be Giroud, with a clever glancing header. 2–1 to France!

When the ball landed in the net, some of the England players held their heads in despair, but not Jude. He never gave up, no matter what. There were still at least fifteen minutes to go – plenty of time to grab another equaliser...

When Jude got the ball near the halfway line, he looked up quickly and spotted substitute Mason on the move. PING! His long pass was perfect, but as Mason tried to control it, he was barged over in the box.

'Penalty!' Jude and his teammates screamed again, and after a VAR check, the referee pointed to the spot.

Yessssssssssssssssssssssssss!

This was it: England's chance to equalise. As Harry stepped up to take it, he looked as calm as ever, but with the pressure on, he went for too much power and blazed it over the bar.

Nooooooooooooooooooooo!

It was a massive miss at a crucial moment, but while Harry stood there alone and devastated, one of his teammates rushed over to comfort him. Guess who? Yes, Jude, England's youngest player.

'Come on, you can still win us this game!' he encouraged his captain.

But despite Jude's encouraging words, it just wasn't England's night. Soon, the final whistle blew, and France were the winners, going through to the World Cup semi-finals.

England, meanwhile, were out. As the news began to sink in, Jude collapsed on the grass, with tears streaming down his face.

'This one will be painful for a very long time,' he posted the day after England's exit. 'The better team on the night went out, that's football sometimes.'

It wasn't all doom and gloom, though. The Three Lions had narrowly lost to the World Champions in a hard-fought battle, and they would all learn a lot from the experience, especially the younger players like Jude.

In just two years, he had gone from the Championship to the Champions League, and from a sub at the Euros to a World Cup superstar. Tackling, running, dribbling, passing, shooting – the boy from Birmingham could do it all, and he did it with such energy, determination, and the will to win. Yes, with a world-class leader like him, the future looked very bright indeed for England.

Jude ended his emotional message with a promise to the fans, and to himself: 'Keep the faith, our time will come.'

At Euro 2024, perhaps? Well first, England would have to qualify...

PART 2

ENGLAND EXCELLENCE, DORTMUND DESPAIR

England kicked off their qualification campaign with a tricky away game against Italy. Could the Three Lions get sweet revenge for their defeat in the Euros final two years earlier? Their line-up was almost exactly the same as last time, with just one major change in midfield: Jude! On that painful night at Wembley, he had watched helplessly from the bench, but now he was out there starting every match for his country, and he was determined to make a difference.

When England won the ball back on the edge of their own box, ZOOM! Jude was off on the counterattack, calling for a quick pass. Instead,

Bukayo curled the ball infield to Harry, who laid it across to Jack Grealish, but Jude kept running until eventually the pass arrived.

What now? As he dribbled towards the box, the Italian defenders backed away, so Jude decided to go for goal himself. BANG! He blasted the ball with plenty of power, but Gigi Donnarumma managed to tip it over the bar. Oooooooh, so close to his second international goal!

Never mind – England took the lead a minute later, and it was Declan, his midfield mate, who scored it. 'Come onnnn!' Jude roared as he raced over to join the team celebrations.

Before half-time, Harry made it 2–0 from the penalty spot, but just when it looked like the Three Lions were cruising to victory, Italy fought back. With three quick passes, they sliced through the England defence and Mateo Retegui slotted home. 2–1 – game on!

And things got even more nerve-wracking when Luke was sent off with fifteen minutes still to go. Suddenly, Jude had to stop attacking and show the other side of his game: his discipline and defensive skills. With brave blocks, tackles and interceptions, he helped England to hold on for an excellent win.

That was only England's first step towards Euro qualification, though. Three days later, they were back in action against Ukraine, and Jude was back in midfield, putting on another all-round masterclass. Harry and Bukayo got the goals, but England's new Number 10 was involved in everything good.

Jude rushed around the pitch intercepting passes and putting the Ukraine defenders under lots of pressure, and he made brilliant bursting runs into dangerous attacking positions.

Then once he got the ball, he created chances for his teammates... and best of all, he skilled his way past two opponents in a tight space with a clever touch, followed by a cheeky nutmeg.

What an impressive performance from Jude, and he was still only nineteen! He was loving life in the England team, but he was never going to relax and lose his football focus. 'There's still so much I've still got to learn,' he said after the Ukraine game.

Really? Like what, Jude? How to create more magic in and around the box, apparently. 'To be honest I think I could have done that a little bit better today. I felt I was a yard or two away from where I needed to be. But it's all experience.'

And in terms of the team, it had been a perfect week. Two tough matches, two excellent England wins – job well done! Now, it was time for Jude to get back to his German club, Borussia Dortmund.

Despite losing their other bright young superstars Jadon Sancho and Erling Haaland, BVB were still battling Bayern Munich for the Bundesliga title. In fact, Jude and his teammates were actually top of the league, above their rivals by one single point. And what was their next match? Bayern away!

A draw would have been a decent result for Dortmund, but instead, it turned into a total disaster. Early on, Jude could only watch in shock and horror as their goalkeeper Gregor Kobel went to clear the ball, completely missed his kick, and it rolled into his own net.

Noooooooooo, what on earth had just happened?!

Ten minutes and a few more mistakes later, Dortmund were 3–0 down. Uh-oh, it was getting embarrassing – what were they going to do now? One thing was for sure: Jude wasn't giving up. He kept pushing forward until eventually, he won a penalty, which Emre Can scored. Donyell Malen continued the late fightback, but it still finished 4–2 to Bayern.

So, was that title race over? No, there was time for plenty more twists and turns ahead. Jude wrote, '7 finals left, we'll give everything!' after helping Dortmund beat Union Berlin. All they could do was keep winning, and hope that Bayern slipped up...

Their wish came true. In their last home match of the season, Bayern lost 3–1 to RB Leipzig, which meant that with one game to go, it was all in Dortmund's hands. If they could just beat Mainz at home on the final day, the Bundesliga title would be theirs for the first time since 2012!

There was only one problem, and it was a pretty major one: Dortmund would have to win it without Jude. He had injured his knee against Borussia

Mönchengladbach, and so sadly the best he could do
was sit on the subs bench.

'Come on, we can do this!' Jude told his
teammates in the dressing room before kick-off.
He could tell that they were feeling the pressure,
but nerves weren't going to help them win. What
Dortmund needed was a strong, confident start.
Instead, however, it turned into another total disaster.

Big mistakes? Tick!

A missed penalty? Tick!

Noooooooooo! Jude couldn't believe what he was
seeing. After twenty-five minutes, Dortmund were
2–0 down, and it stayed that way until the seventieth
minute, when Raphaël Guerreiro finally pulled a goal
back. Okay – game on?

'Let's goooooo!' Jude cheered his teammates on
from the touchline, while handing out water bottles
to anyone who was thirsty.

Dortmund did eventually grab an equaliser, but
there wasn't time to score again. Would a 2–2 draw
be enough to win the league title?

No, Bayern had beaten 1.FC Köln, and so the top

of the table looked like this:

		Points	Goal Difference
1.	Bayern Munich	71	+54
2.	Borussia Dortmund	71	+39

Bayern were the German Champions again... on goal difference!

For Dortmund, it was devastating to come so close to glory, and finish second. All over the pitch, their players fell to the ground in despair. Jude, meanwhile, walked around in his full kit, clapping the fans and wiping the tears from his face.

The disappointment would last for a long time, but at least Jude knew that he had done everything he could for Dortmund: thirty-one games, eight goals, five assists, and one shiny Bundesliga Player of the Season award.

So, was this the end, the right time to say goodbye? It was set to be a very exciting summer for Jude...

PART 3

A GOALSCORING GALÁCTICO

Manchester City, Real Madrid, Liverpool, PSG, Manchester United... Jude was wanted by all of the world's biggest clubs, but which one would he choose to join? By mid-June, he was ready to reveal his big decision, but first, he needed to say an emotional goodbye.

'Thank you to everyone at BVB and to the fans for everything over the past 3 years,' Jude wrote on social media. 'It's been an honour to wear your jersey.'

So, which jersey would he be wearing next season? The answer was... Real Madrid! For a fee of nearly £90 million, Jude would become a new Galáctico!

'It is the proudest day of my life to join the greatest

club in the history of the game,' he announced, while posing for photos with the famous white shirt.

And which number he had chosen for the back?

Not 22 as he'd worn at Birmingham and Dortmund – at Real, that shirt belonged to Antonio Rüdiger.

Not 10 as he often wore for England – at Real, that shirt belonged to Luka Modrić.

No, Jude would be wearing Number 5, the same number as an old club legend and one of his ultimate football heroes, Zinedine Zidane.

It was a lot to live up to, but Jude was confident that he could do it. There was just one crucial question: what position would he play?

A defensive 6,

A box-to-box 8,

Or an attacking 10?

Real already had a long list of midfield maestros: Luka, Toni Kroos, Federico Valverde, Aurélien Tchouaméni, Eduardo Camavinga, Dani Ceballos...

Did they really need another, though? No, what the club needed was a new goalscorer because their star striker Karim Benzema had just moved to Saudi

Arabia. But was Jude really the right man for that job? His Dortmund record wasn't exactly deadly: twenty-four goals in 132 games.

Jude's Real manager, however, had spotted something special. Yes, Jude could do it all in midfield, but Carlo Ancelotti believed that the youngster was at his best further forward in attack. There, he had the power to make bursting runs into the box, the skill to dribble past players, and most importantly, the striker's instinct to score lots of goals. So, when the new season started and Jude made his Real Madrid debut against Athletic Bilbao, he was picked as part of the front three, not the midfield three:

Vinícius Júnior on the left, Rodrygo on the right, and Jude through the middle.

On paper, it looked like a really exciting new attack, but would it work on the pitch? Would Jude be able to adapt to his new role and shine for Real Madrid straight away?

The answer was a big 'YES!' to both questions. Rodrygo made it 1–0 after twenty-eight minutes, and soon it was 2–0. As David Alaba's high corner floated towards him, Jude watched the ball carefully, all the way onto his right boot. He didn't go for a full-power blast, though; he calmly and cleverly kicked the ball into the ground so that it bounced up over the keeper and into the net.

Goooooooooooooooooooooaaaaaaaaaaaaaaaaallllllllllllllll lllllllllllll!!!!!!!!!!!!!!!!!!!!!!!

Jude's heart was racing with excitement, but he didn't show it as he jogged away to celebrate. Standing in front of the fans, he threw his arms out wide. He had arrived: Real Madrid's new goalscoring Galáctico!

After that goal on his Real Madrid debut, Jude just couldn't stop scoring:

Two against Almería – a quick-reaction rebound followed by a flick header on the run…

One against Celta Vigo – a last-minute header to win the game…

…And one against Getafe – another late winning goal, this time with his weaker left foot.

'Yesssss, you hero!' Rodrygo and Nacho cheered as they both jumped on Jude's back.

Wow, what a start to life in Spain! No Real Madrid player had scored in each of his first four league games since... Cristiano Ronaldo!

Jude was loving his new attacking role, and when the Champions League kicked off, he carried on his red-hot form:

A tap-in against Union Berlin...

Then a stunning solo goal against Napoli...

Two in two, and he had a total of eight Real Madrid goals already!

Jude was on fire for his new club – now, could he play the same role for his country?

In a recent friendly match against British rivals Scotland, Jude had been absolutely brilliant, England's man of the match by far. After blasting the ball into the net himself in the first half, he had then set up Harry in the second with an excellent run and pass.

'Mate, that was magic!' Kalvin Phillips yelled, grabbing hold of his teammate for a hug.

Goal? Tick! Assist? Tick! Playing further forward as more of an attacker than a midfielder, Jude felt and looked unstoppable – but now, could he do the same in international matches that really mattered, and help send England to the Euros?

FIRING ENGLAND TO THE EUROS!

17 October 2023

A sold-out Wembley Stadium, with over 83,000 excited fans cheering them on – it was all set to be another massive night for the Three Lions, but as Jude walked out onto the pitch with his teammates, he didn't look around and take in the atmosphere. Instead, he looked straight ahead with total focus. He had an important job to do.

After two more victories and a draw, England were now just one win away from qualifying for Euro 2024. Could they do it tonight, in front of a home crowd against Italy? That was the plan, and Jude was determined to play his part. With his man-of-the-match performance against Scotland he had shown that he was ready to shine for his country in the same way he did for his club, with lots of key goals and assists.

'Come onnnn!' Jude clapped and cheered at the end of the national anthem. He couldn't wait for kick-off.

It was Italy, however, who started the game the strongest. In the fifteenth minute, they broke through the England press and Gianluca Scamacca fired a shot past Jordan Pickford. 1–0! Wembley was stunned into silence, and the players looked shocked too. Oh dear, this wasn't how the game was supposed to go – would England's Euro qualification have to wait until their next match against Malta?

What the Three Lions needed was a creative spark to get them going, and guess who provided it? Jude, their terrific new Number 10! When Declan passed the ball through to him, he flicked it on first time to Harry, and then turned and rushed forward for the one-two. When it arrived, Jude burst away from two Italians and into the box, where a defender slid in...

and fouled him.

'Penalty!' screamed Jude along with all of his England teammates. Yes, the referee pointed to the spot, and up stepped Harry to score. 1–1!

Watching from the edge of the penalty area, Jude raised his fist and punched the air. England were back in the game, and it was all thanks to him. Now, for another moment of magic...

As England searched for a winning goal, Jude was everywhere, and involved in everything. One minute he was on the attack, picking out Phil with a clever diagonal pass, and the next he was back in defence, sliding in to make a crucial tackle. And he didn't stop there.

'YESSSS!' Jude called out as he got back to his feet, and Phil fed him the ball brilliantly. Right – time for the quick counterattack! He could see a defender charging towards him, so Jude flicked the ball past him and then chased after it, determined to reach it first. When he did, he passed it left to Marcus Rashford, who cut inside and blasted a shot into the bottom corner. 2–1!

'Come onnnnnn!' Jude roared, pumping his fists

in front of the ecstatic England fans. At last, they were winning – surely, they were on their way to the Euros now!

It was hugs and high-fives all round for England's two goal heroes: Marcus, who had finished the move off in style, and Jude, whose hard work, speed and skill had created the chance in the first place. With his increasing confidence, what a box-to-box superstar he was becoming!

And even though they were now winning, Jude always wanted to do more for his team.

Out on the right wing, he seemed to be surrounded, but no he still managed to pass the ball to Harry with a silky backheel.

Olé!

He controlled Jordan's long kick with a perfect touch, turned away from danger, and then calmly looked up to find the best pass to play.

Lovely stuff, Jude!

Moving into the middle, he poked a one-two back to Phil, but his shot flew straight at the keeper.

Unlucky!

In the seventy-seventh minute, Harry made it 3–1 to England. Soon after that, after eighty-five minutes, it was time for Jude to take a bow and then a well-deserved rest. He had:

3 successful dribbles…

3 interceptions…

2 assists…

…And 1 more Man of the Match Award coming his way!

As Jude walked off, the fans clapped him all the way, and Jude clapped them right back, with his hands raised above his head. He felt so proud to represent his country on the football pitch.

So, job done for Jude and his teammates? Yes, when the final whistle blew, England had the victory they needed – they had officially qualified for Euro 2024!

But really, that was only the first half of the task, and the players were already looking ahead to the trickier second half: going all the way and winning the tournament in Germany!

At Euro 2020, England had come so close to lifting the trophy, only losing the final on penalties.

Four years on, the team looked better and stronger, especially with their new Number 10 at the centre of everything.

So, would young Jude prove to be the missing piece in the England trophy-winning puzzle? Only time would tell, but the signs looked very exciting indeed. Whether he played in midfield or attack, Jude was a superstar who could make a match-winning difference.

KYLIAN
MBAPPÉ

PART 1

AN UNFORGETTABLE WORLD CUP FINAL

17 October 2023

It was all set to be a sensational end to the 2022 World Cup: Argentina versus the reigning champions, France. There could only be one winner, but who would it be, Lionel Messi the Master or Kylian Mbappé, football's next great superstar?

Kylian certainly looked confident as the two teams lined up in the tunnel before kick-off. He gave Antoine Griezmann a friendly hug, he fist-bumped with a mascot, he winked at the TV camera, and he even shared a smile with Messi!

Wow – Kylian seemed like the calmest person in the

whole stadium, and he had every reason to feel calm and confident. Not only had he already won the World Cup with France back in 2018, but he was also in even better form this time around:

A header against Australia...

Both goals against Denmark...

...And then two more super-strikes against Poland, in a match they were calling 'The Mbappé Show'!

With one game to go, Kylian was the tournament's joint top scorer, tied with... yep, you guessed it, Messi. Let their final battle begin!

At club level, Kylian and Messi were PSG teammates, but for their countries, they were fierce rivals fighting for football's biggest prize. At the 2018 World Cup, young Kylian had terrorised Argentina with his speed and skill, but La Albiceleste were a totally different team now. While Messi was still their leader, he wasn't their only superstar anymore. Ángel Di María, Julián Álvarez, Enzo Fernández, Alexis Mac Allister, Lautaro Martínez – they were all fantastic players that France would have to watch out for.

And which France player would Argentina be

watching out for in particular? Kylian, of course!
Every time he touched the ball, he found at least two
defenders in front of him, who were happy to foul him
if they had to. He tried his best to dribble past them
and set up chances for the other France forwards, but
there was just no way through!

The worst part for Kylian was that, while he got
more and more frustrated at one end of the pitch,
Messi got more and more involved at the other. First,
he scored a penalty, and then he started the move
that ended with Di María scoring a second goal for
Argentina: 2–0!

Noooo! Kylian couldn't believe what he was seeing
from his France teammates. Where was their passion,
their energy, their organisation? Even some harsh
words from their manager at half-time didn't seem
to do much good. With fifteen minutes to go, France
were still 2–0 down and heading for defeat. Kylian,
however, hadn't given up hope. All they needed was
one goal, and they would be back in the game...

At last, a golden chance arrived. As Randal Kolo
Muani raced on to Kylian's clever through-ball, he

was fouled by an Argentina defender. Penalty! Kylian stepped up and calmly buried his shot in the bottom corner. 2–1, game on! Kylian sprinted back to the halfway line with the ball tucked under one arm and his other arm punching the air. *Allez les Bleus!*

France still had plenty of time left to find an equaliser, but in fact it didn't take them long at all because their superstar Number 10 had come alive. Just seconds after the restart, Adrien Rabiot floated a long pass towards Kylian…

Who headed it down to Randal…

Who lobbed the ball over a defender for the one-two with Kylian…

…Who slid in to score on the volley.

Gooooooooooooooooooooaaaaaaaaaaaaaaaalllllllllllllll llllllllllll!!!!!!!!!!!!!!!!!!!

What a strike! This time, Kylian could celebrate properly. He raced away with his arms out wide, and then stood in front of the fans for ages, roaring with passion and relief. Thanks to his two goals, France were still in the World Cup final! Now, could they go on and win it?

The battle of football's biggest superstars continued. When Messi tapped in early in extra time, the France fans feared the worst, but Kylian kept going. Ten minutes later, he controlled the ball on the edge of the box and curled a powerful shot that struck the arm of an Argentina player.

'Handball, PENALTY!' he screamed and the referee pointed to the spot. With even more pressure on his young shoulders, Kylian stepped up again and... calmly buried another shot in the same bottom corner. 3–3!

Wow, Kylian had just scored a hat-trick in the World Cup final to save the day for France! Over by the corner flag, he stopped to do his classic celebration, but as he folded his arms across his chest, he couldn't keep cool like normal, not after an amazing moment like that. So instead, he stuck his tongue out for the cameras. What a final, and what a feeling!

Kylian's heroic work wasn't done yet, though. After 120 minutes of thrilling football, the World Cup trophy would be decided in the most dramatic way possible: penalties!

'I'll take the first one,' he told his teammates in the huddle. Scoring a third penalty in the same game, against the same goalkeeper? No problem, Kylian walked forward with confidence and calmly buried another shot in the same bottom corner!

But anything Kylian could do, Messi could do too. France 1 Argentina 1.

Right, now it was over to the other players. All Kylian could do was watch anxiously from the halfway line, as his teammates stepped up and... missed:

Noooooo! Kingsley Coman's shot was saved by Martínez.

Noooooo! Aurélien Tchouaméni dragged his shot wide.

'Unlucky, it's not over yet!' Kylian clapped and cheered, trying to keep the team spirits up, but soon Gonzalo Montiel had the chance to win it and... he scored. Argentina were the new World Champions!

NOOOOOO! As the Argentina players celebrated around him, Kylian stood there alone, a hand over his mouth, frozen in disappointment. Argghh, France had come so close to lifting the trophy again – losing on penalties was such a painful blow to take, especially after fighting back from 2–0 down. He had given absolutely everything for his country, but in the end, not even three goals (plus a penalty in the shoot-out) had been enough.

Everyone did their best to console Kylian – the Argentina players, his own teammates, his manager, even the French President Emmanuel Macron – but there was nothing they could say to make him feel better. In that moment, it was impossible for him to focus on the positives, even though there were lots of them, most importantly:

1) He had just played a crucial part in an unforgettable World Cup final, perhaps the greatest of all time.

2) He had just won the World Cup Golden Boot, after scoring eight goals.

3) He was still only twenty-three years old!

With everything that he had already achieved in football, it was easy to forget all that. Kylian still had plenty more major tournaments ahead of him for France, and so the next day, he sent a two-word message to his fans:

'Nous reviendrons.' ('We'll come back.')

First step: qualifying for Euro 2024…

PART 2

CAPTAIN KYLIAN

France were expected to reach Euro 2024 with ease, but they would have to do it without two of their most experienced players. Soon after the World Cup 2022 final, their captain and goalkeeper Hugo Lloris had retired from international football, and a month later, so had vice-captain and centre-back Raphaël Varane. Between the two of them, they had won over 230 caps for their country. So, who would France's new leaders be?

There were two names at the top of the list:

Antoine Griezmann,

And Kylian.

One was an attacking midfielder, the other was a

forward. One was thirty-one years old, the other was twenty-four. One had over 110 caps for France, the other sixty-five.

It was a classic case of experience versus youth, but which player would the manager pick to wear the precious armband? In March 2023, with France's first Euro qualifiers just a few days away, Deschamps finally announced his big decision: 'Mbappé will be our captain.'

Wow, thanks Boss – what a proud moment! Kylian couldn't wait to get started in his new role, with Antoine alongside him as vice-captain. But would the extra responsibility change the way Kylian played on the pitch? No, no, no, and he was about to prove it straight away.

France's Euro qualification kicked off with a tough match against the Netherlands. The Dutch had talented players all over the pitch, but they were especially strong in defence. With Bayern Munich's Matthijs de Ligt, Liverpool's Virgil van Dijk, Nathan Aké of Manchester City – oof, this Dutch line-up was going to be a real test for France's forwards!

Kylian, however, was desperate to impress in his first game as national captain. After leading his team out on to the pitch at the Stade de France, his next task was leading them to a fantastic victory. Challenge accepted! In fact, it only took two minutes for France's two new leaders to link up for a goal. From wide on the left wing, Kylian passed the ball across to Antoine, who found the net with a first-time strike. 1–0!

'Yesssss!' Antoine yelled, pointing and running towards his teammate to thank him for the assist.

What a start, and the France goals kept coming. First, Dayot Upamecano bundled the ball in from an Antoine free kick, and then it was Kylian's turn to score. After laying it back to Aurélien near the halfway line, ZOOM! he was off, sprinting in between two Dutch defenders and towards the box at top speed.

It was a very difficult pass to play, but Aurélien managed it, with a little help from Randal's clever dummy. As the ball rolled all the way through to Kylian, there was only going to be one result:

Gooooooooooooooooooooaaaaaaaaaaaaaaaalllllllllllllll llllllllllll!!!!!!!!!!!!!!!!!!

Nerve-wracking new role, same calm finishing – Kylian was loving life as France's leader, and as he celebrated, he made sure to thank his excellent teammates.

For his second goal of the game, however, Kylian didn't need much help from anyone else. From the middle of the Dutch half, he dribbled forward, past one tackle, then another, before firing an unstoppable shot into the bottom corner. 4–0!

Whoa – the captain's armband seemed to suit Kylian very well indeed! 'Nothing better to start a new era,' he posted on social media afterwards. 'A great win for the team.'

Next up for France: an away trip to Ireland. The atmosphere at the Aviva Stadium was famously aggressive, and their opponents would probably be set up very defensively to play for the draw. It was going to be a different kind of challenge for Kylian and his teammates, but they would just have to find a way to win...

As it turned out, patience was the key. France created so many chances in the first half alone, but somehow not one of them went in.

Nathan Collins hooked the ball away just as Kylian was about to strike it... and then John Egan cleared Kylian's cross just before it reached Olivier Giroud.

A few minutes later, Olivier's header hit one defender, then another, before bouncing safely into the keeper's gloves... and then Antoine's header flew wide.

Half-time score: 0–0! How?

The France players returned to the dressing room feeling frustrated, but it was important that they didn't get too frustrated. As Kylian reminded them in his captain's speech, they still had plenty of time to score.

'Come on, keep your heads up – we've got the whole second half ahead of us!'

But when the game restarted, it was the same old story for France. Wide on the left wing, Kylian twisted and turned with the ball at his feet, waiting for something special to happen, like a teammate making a run, or a gap appearing in the Irish defence. But no, there was nothing, so he played it down the line to Adrien, who lost possession with a sloppy pass.

Arghhhh, not good enough! But just as Kylian was starting to get fed up, France scored a goal out of nowhere. Their right-back Benjamin Pavard rushed in to intercept a pass, and then unleashed a rocket of a shot that flew over the keeper and crashed in off the crossbar. At last: 1–0!

As Benjamin slid towards the corner flag on his knees, his captain was the first player to reach him.

'Benji, you hero!' Kylian cried out, giving him a great big hug.

When the final whistle blew, their goalscorer got even more hugs because his stunning strike turned out to be the winner. Phew! No, France hadn't played as well as they had at home against the Netherlands, but they were a young team learning together, and what mattered most was the results.

Two matches, two victories – Captain Kylian was off to a winning start.

PART 3

A BRIGHT FUTURE FOR FRANCE

As talented as their players were, France were still a young team going through major changes all over the pitch.

In goal, they had said goodbye to Hugo, and hello to Mike Maignan.

Defenders Raphaël and Presnel Kimpembe had been replaced by Dayot, Ibrahima Konaté and William Saliba.

In midfield, there was no more Paul Pogba or N'Golo Kanté; it was all about Aurélien, Adrien and Eduardo Camavinga now.

And up front, despite losing Karim Benzema, France had more exciting forwards than ever to choose from:

Randal,

Kingsley,

Ousmane Dembélé,

Marcus Thuram,

Moussa Diaby,

Christopher Nkunku...

...And of course, the most exciting of all, Captain Kylian!

For his club, PSG, Kylian was now part of an all-French front three, alongside Randal and Ousmane. Together, were they the future of the France national team? It certainly seemed that way, but it was still early days. They hadn't even qualified for Euro 2024 yet!

But with each hard-fought win, they were getting closer and closer:

Gibraltar 0–3 France.

Kylian scored a penalty just before half-time, to calm the fears of the fans.

France 1–0 Greece.

Another game, another crucial Kylian penalty. This time, however, he needed a second chance to score.

His first attempt was saved but VAR decided that a Greek defender had entered the box before he kicked the ball, and so he was allowed to take it again. What now – should he go for the same side again? No, after a stuttering run-up, Kylian blasted the ball into the opposite corner of the net instead.

Goooooooooooooooooooooaaaaaaaaaaaaaaaaalllllllllllllll llllllllllll!!!!!!!!!!!!!!!!!!!!!

'Come onnnnnn!' Kylian roared as he jumped up and punched the air. That penalty was his fifty-fourth goal of the 2022–23 season for club and country, beating the previous best of fifty-three scored by French striker Just Fontaine in 1957–58.

Even though the new France team was still struggling to find their top form, Kylian was still the same old Kylian, scoring goals and breaking records. And thanks to him, they were still winning all their matches along the way. With four victories out of four, Les Bleus were already six points clear at the top of Euro Qualification Group B. Two more wins and they would be on their way to Germany...

France 2–0 Ireland.

For once, Kylian didn't score, but he still played a leading part for his country. When a clearance bounced out to him on the edge of the box, he thought about shooting for goal himself. But instead he shifted the ball back to Aurélien, who had the space and skill to curl a powerful shot into the bottom corner. 1–0!

'Whoa, what a strike!' Kylian cried out, chasing after his teammate. As captain, it was exactly what he wanted to see: the younger players stepping up and showing what they could really do.

Early in the second half, France scored an even better goal, with a fast, flowing team move. From the right, Ousmane passed the ball inside Antoine...

Who threaded it through to Randal...

Who flicked it back to Antoine...

Who spread the ball left to Theo Hernández...

...Who crossed it in for Kylian. BANG! His shot was blocked, but the rebound fell to Marcus, who spun brilliantly to score. 2–0!

'Yesssssss, that's more like it!' Captain Kylian cheered while the whole team celebrated together in a big huddle.

A few days later, he posted a photo of himself laughing at training, and underneath he wrote the words 'Happy kid'. It was true. He was having loads of fun, and suddenly, the future looked very bright indeed for France:

Their defence was so strong that they hadn't conceded a single goal in five games;

Their midfield was looking balanced and brilliant;

Their forwards were starting to fire together at last;

And a place at Euro 2024 was now only one more win away...

PART 4

GERMANY, HERE WE GO!

13 October 2023

One more win – that was all France needed as they travelled to Amsterdam to take on the Netherlands again. Could they book their spot at Euro 2024 with two games to spare? That was the aim, and the match would also be the perfect way to test how much progress they had made together.

'Come onnnnnnnn!' Kylian clapped and cheered during his last stretches before kick-off. He was raring to go, but what about the others? Oh yes – they were feeling it too, and in the sixth minute, France took the lead after another fast, flowing team move.

On the right wing, Kingsley played a one-two with Jonathan Clauss and then burst into the box. When two defenders closed him down, he laid the ball back to Antoine...

Who fired a first-time pass through to Jonathan...

...Who crossed it in towards... Kylian! He was being tightly marked by the young Dutch defender Lutsharel Geertruida, but he used his strength and speed to beat him to the ball. BANG! Kylian struck it on the volley, and his shot flew over the keeper and into the net. 1–0!

Goooooooooooooooooooaaaaaaaaaaaaaaaaalllllllllllllll lllllllllll!!!!!!!!!!!!!!!!!!!

Yessss, France were winning already! As Kylian stood there pointing up at the sky with both hands, he was soon surrounded by his teammates. Hurray, together, they were heading for Euro 2024!

The rest of the first half was an even contest, with chances for both teams, but early in the second, France scored again to settle any nerves, and guess who got the goal?

It all started with an overhit cross from Kingsley that

was headed away as far as Theo. When he passed the ball to Kylian, wide on the left wing, it didn't look like a particularly dangerous situation, but with a sudden burst of energy, France's captain came alive.

PING! Kylian played a quick pass through to Adrien, and then kept sprinting forward.

TAP! Adrien flicked the ball through into Kylian's path.

BANG! From just outside the box, Kylian curled an unstoppable shot into the top corner. 2–0!

Goooooooooooooooooooooaaaaaaaaaaaaaaaalllllllllllllll lllllllllllll!!!!!!!!!!!!!!!!!!!

'Whoa, what a hit!' Antoine shouted as he chased after Kylian. He had seen him do so many special things that nothing really surprised him anymore.

But surely that had to be one of the best goals that Kylian had ever scored, for club or country! And it was a significant one too – his forty-second for France. He had already overtaken several national heroes – Karim, David Trezeguet, Zinedine Zidane – and with that wondergoal, he had just moved past another: Michel Platini. There were now only three players left ahead of him on the list:

Antoine, with forty-four goals…

Thierry Henry, with fifty-one…

…And Olivier, with fifty-six.

Challenge accepted – if he kept it up, Kylian would be his country's leading goalscorer in no time!

The most important thing, however, was the team, and thanks to him, France were flying towards another major tournament. With ten minutes to go, the Netherlands did pull one goal back, but they couldn't stop Kylian and his match-winning machine…

'Germany, here we go!'

When the final whistle blew, some of the France players jumped for joy, but not their captain. Kylian hardly even smiled as he walked around the pitch, shaking hands. Because while qualifying for Euro 2024 was an important first step, they hadn't achieved anything yet.

So, now that they were officially on their way to Germany, would France relax and take it easy? No, no, no! Their next match against Scotland was meant to be a friendly, but Kylian always took his football seriously.

With a silky stepover, he escaped from his marker and delivered a perfect cross to Benjamin. 2–1!

Then fifteen minutes later, he stepped up to score a goal of his own from the penalty spot. 3–1!

Poor Gibraltar were the next team to suffer. At half-time, France were already 7–0 up, and it finished 14–0, with two hat-tricks for Kylian: one of assists, and one of goals.

As his goals total rose to forty-four, forty-five, forty-six, he was now ahead of Antoine, and only five behind Henry. If he had an excellent Euro 2024, Kylian knew that he could easily score those five goals to equal Henry's record, if not more. That was his target, as well as leading his country all the way to the trophy this time.

In the Euro 2020 championships, France had suffered a shock defeat to Switzerland in the Round of 16, and it was Kylian who had missed the crucial penalty in the shoot-out. Despite his best efforts, he hadn't been able to make amends by winning the 2022 World Cup for France. But what about the forthcoming Euro 2024? It wouldn't be easy against top teams like England, Germany and Spain, but with Kylian on the pitch, Les Bleus truly believed that they could beat anyone.

ANDY ROBERTSON

PART 1

WATCHING THE WORLD CUP FROM HOME

1 June 2022, Hampden Park

During a brief pause in play, Andy took a deep breath and looked up at the big scoreboard in the stadium:

'83:47

SCOTLAND 1 UKRAINE 2'

Argghh, why was the time ticking by so fast?! Unless they could find another goal soon, Scotland's World Cup dream would be over...

Andy shook his head and sighed; this really wasn't how this game was supposed to go. They had worked so hard to finish second in their qualifying group and earn a home tie in the play-off semi-finals. The Tartan

Army, The Hampden Roar – the idea was that their
incredible supporters would help inspire Scotland
to victory, and take them through to the final, one
game away from their first World Cup since 1998. But
instead, in their biggest game in years, the team had
frozen and let the occasion get the better of them.

There was still time to turn things around, though.
When Stuart Armstrong dribbled up the right wing
and fired a cross into the middle, Andy raced in off
the left to meet it. Was this it for Andy – his big
captain's moment? For his club Liverpool, he was a
flying full-back, but for his country, he often played
further forward as a wing-back, which meant more
opportunities to ATTACK…

So, should he shoot first time or take a touch?
Andy went for the safer, second option, but that was
a mistake because it gave a Ukraine defender time
to close him down. Nooooo! It felt like nothing was
going right for Scotland today.

In the very last minute of injury time, Andy floated
one final cross into the box. Grant Hanley jumped
and won the header, but the ball dropped down to

Oleksandr Zinchenko and suddenly the counterattack was on – uh-oh, four Ukraine attackers against three Scottish defenders! As Zinchenko slipped a pass through to Artem Dovbyk, Andy tried to step up and catch the striker offside, but it didn't work. Dovbyk was off, sprinting towards the Scotland goal, where he shot past Craig Gordon. 3–1!

Noooooooooooo! As he watched the ball hit the back of the net, Andy's head and shoulders dropped and his heart sank. It was game over, World Cup dream over.

In that horrible moment, all Andy wanted to do was go home and hide away, but as the Scotland captain, it was his job to stand in front of the TV cameras and speak for his team.

'It's hugely disappointing as we've waited a long time for this game,' Andy said honestly with a glum look on his face. 'After a really positive campaign, we've let ourselves down tonight.'

Sadly, the pain got worse before it got better. Four days later, Scotland's British rivals Wales beat Ukraine 1–0 in the play-off finals to reach their first World Cup since 1958. Andy couldn't help thinking, 'Arghhhh, that should have been us!'

Oh well – at least, after some time away from football with his family, Andy was able to look back and see the progress his Scotland team had made together. Under their manager Steve Clarke, they had already come so far, from losing to Georgia and Kazakhstan, to beating Austria and Denmark. Their World Cup dream hadn't worked out this time, but there were lots more major tournaments ahead. They just had to stick together and keep improving.

Before the World Cup even kicked off in Qatar, Scotland had already started bouncing back. In the UEFA Nations League, they were placed in a group with Armenia, the Republic of Ireland... and Ukraine! Yes, they would have a chance to put that play-off disappointment behind them straight away. Sadly, Andy had to miss the home match at Hampden because of a knee injury, but Scotland were magnificent without him.

First Super John McGinn shrugged off a Ukraine defender and fired a shot into the bottom corner. 1–0!

Then Lyndon Dykes came on and scored two late

headers from Ryan Fraser corners. 2–0, 3–0!

Get in – what a performance! Andy was so proud of his players. 'That's more like it, lads!' he messaged them all.

That win made the experience of watching the World Cup from home a little bit easier. Sometimes, Andy couldn't help wondering 'What if?', especially when Wales played England in the group stage, but mostly, he tried to stay positive, and see the tournament as motivation for the future.

'Next time, we're gonna be there, mate!' Andy told Stuart confidently.

But first, there was another major international tournament for Scotland to get excited about: Euro 2024 in Germany. They had successfully qualified before – for the 2020 Euros – and that was the aim again, although their path looked more complicated this time around. To get there, they would have to finish as one of the top two teams in a group that also included:

Pedri's Spain…

Erling Haaland's Norway…

...And Khvicha Kvaratskhelia's Georgia.

'Bring it on!' Andy told his Scotland teammates with a smile.

PART 2

A SPECIAL NIGHT AT HAMPDEN

March 2023

'It's good to be back,' Andy posted on social media with a photo from a very fun-looking training session. Scotland's first Euro qualifiers were now only a few days away, and the team spirit was as strong as ever. They were just a big group of friends who loved meeting up and winning football matches together.

Match number one: Cyprus at home. Scotland were on top right from the start, but could they turn all their possession into a goal? In the twentieth minute, Kieran Tierney collected the ball in defence, and ZOOM! Andy raced right past him, up the wing, on the overlap. It was the great thing about Scotland having two such brilliant left-backs.

What happened next was a move they'd practised so many times in training: Kieran passed the ball inside to Stuart, who poked a pass through to Andy on the run, who fired it across the six-yard box. The ball flicked up off a Cyprus defender and dropped down perfectly for John at the back post, who calmly volleyed it in. 1–0!

'Come onnnnn!' Andy roared, pounding the grass where he'd slipped over setting the goal up.

'Thanks, Robbo!' John shouted as they shared a hug and a high-five. 'Are you alright?'

Andy smiled. 'Never been better, mate!'

Scotland were up and running on the road to Euro 2024, and they sealed a first victory with two late goals from super-sub Scott McTominay.

In the past, Clarke had mainly used the Manchester United man as a third centre-back, but this time, he came on as an attacking midfielder, and what an impact he made! First, Scott used his power to burst into the box and score, and then he used his skill to calmly guide Andy's pass into the bottom corner. 3–0!

'Good start,' was all Andy said after the game. Scotland couldn't afford to get carried away, not when their next opponents were Spain! Oooooooh – this was the big one, in front of a loud, home crowd at Hampden Park. Could Scotland do what they'd done to Denmark in the 2022 World Cup qualifiers, and pull off a surprise victory?

One thing was for sure: it was going to be very different from the Cyprus game. Against Spain, Scotland would have a lot less of the ball, so when they did get it, they would need to make the most of it...

In the sixth minute, Andy rushed forward to put Pedro Porro under pressure, and as the Spain right-back tried to escape, he suddenly slipped on the edge of his own penalty area. Ooooh, an early chance for Scotland! Andy had to make the most of it. After a quick look up, he cut the ball back for Scott as he burst into the box. BANG! His shot deflected off a defender and flew past the keeper. 1–0!

'Yesssssss!' Andy cheered, throwing both arms in the air. Wow, Scotland were winning already, and he had helped to set the goal up!

They still had a long way to go, though – nearly ninety minutes, in fact. As the game continued, the action moved from end to end, with both teams missing good chances, but at half-time, it was still 1–0 to Scotland. Hurray, they were halfway there!

'Keep going, lads,' Andy clapped and cheered as Scotland took to the field again for the second half, 'and let's take our chances if they come!'

In the fiftieth minute, it was his turn to stay back, while Kieran legged it up the left wing. Once, twice, he sped away from Dani Carvajal, before fizzing a cross towards John in the middle. A Spain defender managed to intercept it, but as the ball bounced up, who was bursting into the box again, ready to blast it into the bottom corner? Yes, it was Scott – 2–0!

Whoa, what on earth was going on? He had now scored four goals in two games for Scotland, and they were beating Spain!

Andy had experienced some very noisy nights at

Hampden before, but nothing quite like this. The atmosphere was amazing; it was as if the stadium was actually rocking! With his arm around Kieran, Scott raced over to the touchline where everyone celebrated together in front of the fans – the starters, the substitutes, the coaches and the manager.

But after enjoying the moment, it was straight back to business.

'Come on, stay focused,' Andy shouted to his teammates. 'We haven't won this yet!'

In the last thirty minutes, Spain attacked again and again, but no matter how much they passed the ball around, they couldn't find a way through the strong Scottish defence. With the home crowd urging them on, Andy and his teammates felt absolutely invincible, and their energy levels were endless.

'*HURRAAAAAAAAAAAAAAAAYYYYYYY!!!!!*'

When the final whistle blew, Hampden let out its loudest roar of the night. What a win! Nothing was going to stop the Scottish celebrations, not the howling wind or the heavy rain. Even Clarke, their manager, was smiling, and that hardly ever happened!

After lots of hugs and handshakes, Andy led
his team of heroes on a lap of honour around the
pitch, to clap all the incredible supporters. What an
important part they had played – Scotland couldn't
have won it without them!

'Special Night at Hampden' – that's how Andy
described it in a message to the fans, and there
would be more of those to come...

PART 3

MOVING CLOSER WITH EVERY MATCH

With two wins out of two, Scotland were off to an excellent start, but they couldn't start thinking ahead to Euro 2024 just yet.

'We've got two massive games in June,' Andy reminded everyone after the victory against Spain, 'and if we come out of that with the points we think we need, we'll be in a good position.'

Norway away, followed by Georgia at home – how many points were Scotland hoping to pick up? Six was always the aim, of course, but a draw against Erling Haaland and Martin Ødegaard wouldn't be such a bad result, would it?

In Oslo, Norway had most of the ball, but they

hardly created any actual goalscoring chances, until suddenly, Haaland came alive in the second half. First, he almost dribbled through the Scotland defence on his own, and then, when a cross came into the box, his clever movement forced Ryan Porteous to pull him back. Penalty!

'No way, ref – he dived!' Ryan tried to argue, but it was no use. Up stepped Haaland himself to place the ball in the bottom corner. 1–0 to Norway!

Oh dear – what were Scotland going to do now? Well, what they weren't going to do was panic. There was no need; they still had plenty of time left, and plenty of talented players to bring off the bench too. So they waited and waited, and then with ten minutes to go, Clarke sent on three super subs: Stuart Armstrong, Billy Gilmour, and Kenny McLean.

'Keep moving the ball around, and a chance will come!' the manager called out to his team.

Yes, Boss! With Norway starting to relax and Haaland off having a rest, Scotland saw their opportunity. Patiently, they passed it forward, from back to front: Jack Hendry to Scott, to John,

to Lyndon? No, the final pass was cut out by Leo
Østigård, but as the ball bounced loose, the Norway
defenders all left it to each other, and Lydon
pounced, poking a shot past the keeper. 1–1!

'Come onnnnnnn!' Andy screamed, punching the
air with both fists. Scotland had done it; they were
back in the game!

Now, should they sit back and settle for the draw,
or push forward for the win? A point was a lot better
than nothing for Scotland, but Andy had a feeling
that now that they'd scored one, they could score
again. After a quick chat with his manager, he had a
message to deliver to his teammates:

'Let's go get another goal!'

Yes, Robbo! Seconds later, Scott led them forward
on another attack. His high, chipped cross floated
over Lyndon's head, but it bounced down in front of
John, on the left side of the box.

'Ooooooooooh!' the Scotland fans gasped, rising
to their feet in a rush. Could they? They couldn't…
could they?

John thought about taking a shot himself, but

instead he crossed it to Lyndon, who laid it back to Kenny…

'Oooooooooh!'

…Who calmly curled the ball into the bottom corner. 2–1!

'HURRAAAAAAAAAAAAAAAYYYYYYY!!!!!!'

Unbelievable, what a turnaround – from 1–0 down to 2–1 up, in just 104 seconds! The Scotland players, coaches and supporters were in dreamland, bouncing up and down together with the biggest smiles on their faces.

Andy was so, so proud of his teammates; they all worked so hard for each other, they never, ever gave up, and look what they had just achieved! First, they had stunned Spain, and now they had beaten Norway too. So, were they now daring to dream of Euro 2024? 'We couldn't have started this campaign much better, but we have to use it to our advantage,' Andy told the journalists. 'We have to qualify now.'

And the only way to qualify was to keep on winning! Yes, Scotland were moving closer with every match.

At home against Georgia, they got the job done swiftly, with no need for late drama this time. On a soaking wet pitch, Callum McGregor gave them the lead early in the first half, and then early in the second, Andy attacked up the left and set up Scott to score again.

'Yesssssssssssss!' Andy roared, along with the rest of Hampden Park. This Scotland team was looking unstoppable!

Could they make it five wins from five, away against Cyprus?

As Che Adams went to take an early throw-in on the left, ZOOM! Andy sprinted forward into space, calling for the ball. When it arrived, he took a touch, looked up, and then did what he did best: curl another incredible cross into the box. He had been doing it consistently for years, for club and country.

At the front post, John could only flick the ball goalwards, but Scott was there yet again to nod it into the net. 1–0!

'When did you become such a goal machine?!' Andy asked while they celebrated together.

'When you started delivering decent crosses!' Scott joked back.

By half-time, Scotland were in total control.

From an Andy free kick, Jack headed the ball down and his fellow defender Ryan Porteous bundled it in. 2–0!

Then Scott dribbled forward and set up John, who curled a shot past the keeper before he could even move. 3–0!

Scotland! Scotland! Scotland!

Their supporters could hardly believe what they were seeing. Was this really the same national team? After so many years of dull football and disappointments, it was a joy to watch a group of Scottish players having so much fun together on the pitch, and most importantly, WINNING MATCHES!

Andy sent an update to his followers: '5/5. One step closer.'

Surely, Scotland were on their way to the Euros?

PART 4

"WE'RE OFF TO GERMANY!"

One point – that was all Scotland now needed as they travelled to Seville for their return match against Spain. Another win would be even better, of course, but they were confident that they could fight for at least a draw.

'And then we'll be off to Germany!' Andy reminded his teammates for the thousandth time.

Spain, however, were also a team on a Euro-qualifying mission. Ferran Torres fired just wide, Mikel Merino hit the post, and then Álvaro Morata had a goal ruled out for offside. Phew! With half-time approaching, Scotland were still hanging on, but all of a sudden, disaster struck...

It all started with a long ball into the box, which
Andy jumped up to try and head. He was up against
the tall Spanish keeper Unai Simón, however, who
came out to catch the ball and collided with Andy,
knocking him to the floor. Owwww!

But that was only the first part of the pain because
as Andy lay there on the grass, Simón then fell on top
of him, crushing his right shoulder in an awkward
position. OWWWW!

Andy knew straight away that the injury was
serious; he was in absolute agony. He stayed down
holding his shoulder until the team doctors arrived,
and after a quick examination, they agreed: there was
no way that he could play on. So, with his right arm
wrapped up in his shirt like a sling, Andy slowly and
sadly made his way over to the touchline. If Scotland
were going to qualify for the Euros, they would have
to do it without their captain.

'Don't worry, Robbo – we've got this!' his
teammates reassured him in the dressing room at half-
time, and in the fifty-eighth minute, it looked like they
were right. From a really tight angle, Scott somehow

curled a free kick into the far corner of the net. 1–0!

Hurrrraaaaaaaaaaaaaayyyyy!

But wait – while the Scotland supporters were going wild, the VAR told the referee to go and look at something on the screen. What, a potential push by Jack on the keeper? It didn't seem clear or obvious, but the referee still ruled, 'NO GOAL!'

Boooooooooooooooooooooo!

After that lucky escape, Spain went on to win the match 2–0 with late goals from Morata and Oihan Sancet. Oh well, Scotland had suffered their first defeat of the campaign, but there was no need for the players to panic. Their Euro 2024 dream was still alive; they would just have to wait a little longer to book their place.

But for how long? Well, their next match, Georgia away, was just over a month away, but there was a good chance that they could qualify before that, without even kicking a ball. If Spain could win or draw their game against Norway three days later, then it would be celebration time for Scotland…

At half-time, the score was still 0–0, but just after

the break, Gavi fired the ball in. Yessssssss, Spain were winning! Forty anxious minutes later, the Scotland team could relax and enjoy a very special moment together: they had officially qualified for Euro 2024!

'What a special group!!!' Andy posted with a picture of all the players. 'SEE YOU IN GERMANY!'

The good news was all the more important for Andy because it helped to ease the pain of the bad news: he was about to miss three months of football for club and country due to his shoulder injury.

'At least I'll be back in plenty of time to get fit for the Euros!' he told Stuart with a smile.

In the meantime, Scotland had a qualification campaign to finish off without their captain. Two games to go! Away in Georgia, they twice came back to draw 2–2, thanks to yet another goal from Scott and then one from one of Andy's oldest football friends. He had first met Lawrence Shankland way back in 2009 when they were both youth team players at Queen's Park – and look at them now, starring for the national team together. Amazing!

Three days later, it was time for Scotland's last

match, which was going to be massive: Norway, at home at Hampden Park. The game itself would be an interesting test against tough opponents, but it was also a chance for the players to celebrate their achievement with the fans afterwards, and that was the main reason why Andy had travelled up from Liverpool to be there.

The match actually turned out to be a 3–3 thriller – and the rest of the night was unforgettable too. First, Andy and all of his teammates and coaches walked out into the middle of the pitch, wearing matching white T-shirts with a four-word message written across them:

'WE'RE OFF TO GERMANY!'

Hurrrraaaaaaaaaaaaaayyyyy!

Then, as they walked around on a lap of honour, the Stadium DJ got the Euro party started, with flashing lights and banging, singalong tunes:

Scotland's on fire,

Your defence is terrified,

Scotland's on fire,

OOO Na na na na na na na na…

SCOTLAND! SCOTLAND! SCOTLAND!

What a night, and what a team! Andy was so proud to be a part of it. He couldn't wait to lead Scotland at Euro 2024, and with more success than last time, hopefully.

While Euro 2020 had been an incredible experience for Scotland, the players had all come away with the same frustrating feeling: 'We could have done better!' A draw against England was always a decent result, but the two defeats against Czech Republic and Croatia had been bitterly disappointing, especially after all that hard work to qualify.

Three games, one point, one goal scored, bottom of the group – not good enough! Andy and his Scotland teammates were determined to do so much better in Germany.

CRISTIANO
RONALDO

PART 1

STILL PORTUGAL'S NO. 1 SUPERSTAR?

As Cristiano arrived in Qatar for his fifth World Cup, the big question on many people's lips was: would this one be his last? The Portuguese legend was now thirty-seven years old, and he had already achieved so much:

Winning Euro 2016,

Winning the 2018–19 UEFA Nations League,

Becoming the leading goalscorer in the history of men's international football…

But there was still one massive thing missing for Cristiano – and for his great rival, Lionel Messi – and that was the World Cup. With his famous will to win, was he really going to retire without winning it?

At Cristiano's first tournament in 2006, Portugal had finished in fourth place, but they hadn't since progressed beyond the Round of 16. For a country blessed with so many talented footballers, that was a big disappointment.

So, what were their chances of winning the 2022 World Cup? Pretty slim, it seemed. Despite having their strongest squad in years, Portugal had only reached the tournament through the play-offs. For the first time, some supporters were even questioning Cristiano's role within the team. Was their ageing captain really so important anymore, when they also had other, younger superstars like Bernardo Silva, Bruno Fernandes, João Félix and Rafael Leão?

When Portugal walked out to play their first World Cup group game against Ghana, however, Cristiano was still there at the front of the line, wearing the captain's armband. And who scored their first goal of the tournament? Yes, Cristiano! In the sixty-fifth minute, he was fouled in the box and blasted home the penalty. 1–0!

Goooooooooooaaaaaaaaaaalllllllllllllll!!!!!!!!!!!!!!!!!

Cristiano raced towards the corner flag with a big grin on his face – not only were Portugal winning, but he had just become the first male player to score in five different World Cups!

After that, it was over to Portugal's other superstars.

First, Bruno slipped a great pass through to João who finished in style. 2–1!

Then Bruno set up Rafael, who slid a shot into the bottom corner. 3–1!

'Well done, guys!' Cristiano congratulated his teammates after the game.

Portugal were off to a promising start, and they followed it up with another impressive performance against Uruguay. This time, Cristiano didn't score his team's first goal, but he still celebrated like he had anyway. Although Bruno's curling cross from the left didn't actually touch his head before bouncing down into the net, that wasn't going to stop Cristiano.

'Yesssss!' he cheered, racing away with his right arm high in the air.

It was Bruno who scored their second goal too, from the penalty spot, after Cristiano had been subbed

off for the second game in a row. Hmmm, interesting!
Was Cristiano still Portugal's Number One superstar,
or was their manager, Fernando Santos, starting to
look towards the future, a future without him?

In their final group game against South Korea,
Cristiano came off even earlier, in the sixty-fifth
minute. By then, Portugal were already through to the
Round of 16, but still, he didn't look very happy as he
walked slowly off the pitch.

At least Cristiano would be back in the team for the
next game against Switzerland... wouldn't he? No,
when Santos announced his starting line-up, there
was a big surprise – Gonçalo Ramos was playing as
Portugal's striker instead!

What?! Was Cristiano injured? No, he was there on
the subs bench.

So, how would Portugal perform without their
captain and No. 1 superstar? The answer was:
magnificently!

João set up Gonçalo, who smashed the ball into the
top corner. 1–0!

Pepe headed home from Bruno's corner. 2–0!

Gonçalo poked Diogo Dalot's cross through the keeper's legs. 3–0!

Raphaël Guerreiro finished off a fantastic team move. 4–0!

João set up Gonçalo again, who lifted a clever shot over the diving keeper. 5–1!

Amazing – Gonçalo had a hat-trick on his full World Cup debut! What a wise decision it now looked from the Portugal manager!

But what about Cristiano? He finally came on in the seventy-fourth minute, with Pepe rushing over to give his captain's armband back. So, was there enough time left for him to grab a sixth goal for Portugal?

After a long run-up, Cristiano fired a free kick... straight at the wall.

He raced onto Rafael's throughball and finished brilliantly... but the goal was ruled out for offside.

He chased after Bernardo's chipped pass... but a defender beat him to the ball.

Eventually, a sixth goal did arrive, but it was Rafael who scored it, not Cristiano. Never mind, the most important thing was that Portugal had won, and they were through to the World Cup quarter-finals for the first time in sixteen years.

'A fantastic show by a team full of talent and youth. Congratulations to our National Team. The dream is alive!' Cristiano wrote on social media. 'Força, Portugal!'

For their next match against Morocco, Santos had a big decision to make – stick with the same team, or bring Cristiano back in? In the end, the manager went for the first option – after all, how could he change such a successful winning side?

The new Portugal started the game well. João almost scored with a diving header, Raphael had a vicious volley blocked, and then João's shot deflected off a defender and flew just over the bar. So close!

But as the minutes ticked by, Morocco grew into the game, and just before half-time, they took the lead. When a cross came in from the left, it was Youssef En-Nesyri who jumped the highest, above the Portugal keeper Diogo Costa, to head the ball home. 1–0!

Uh-oh, was it time for Cristiano? In the fiftieth

minute, Portugal's captain and top scorer stood on the touchline, ready to come on. So, could he make a match-winning impact and save the day for his country once again?

Cristiano called for the ball on the edge of the six-yard box, but Diogo decided to cross it instead. Arghhh!

Bruno lifted a high ball into the middle, but Cristiano couldn't quite reach it. ARGHHH!

Cristiano laid the ball back to João, but his shot was saved. Noooooo!

At last, in the ninetieth minute, Cristiano got a first chance to shoot, but the ball flew straight at the keeper. NOOOOOO!

Soon, it was all over, and Portugal were out of the 2022 World Cup. As he walked off the pitch, Cristiano cried and cried.

'Winning the World Cup for Portugal was the biggest dream of my career,' he wrote in an emotional message to his fans. 'I fought hard for this dream. In the 5 appearances I made in the World Cup over 16 years, always next to great players and

supported by millions of Portuguese, I gave it my all...
Unfortunately, yesterday the dream ended.'

So, was that the end of Cristiano's incredible
international career? No, after a lot of thought, he
decided to carry on playing for one more major
tournament: Euro 2024. That was the plan, as long as:

a) Portugal could qualify,

and

b) he was still picked for the team...

PART 2

NEW MANAGER, SAME INCREDIBLE CAPTAIN

After their World Cup disappointment, Portugal decided to say goodbye to Santos, their manager for the last eight years. It was time to try someone new, but who?

José 'The Special One' Mourinho?

Paulo Fonseca?

The national Under-21s coach, Rui Jorge?

In the end, they went for a foreign manager: the Spaniard Roberto Martínez, who had taken Belgium to third place at the 2018 World Cup. Not only was he a successful international coach, but Martínez also liked his teams to play an attacking style of football, which would hopefully suit Portugal's players a lot better.

And when Martínez named his squad for their first Euro qualifiers, Cristiano was there amongst the forwards.

'Cristiano Ronaldo is a player who is completely committed to the national team,' Portugal's manager said. 'He has the chance to help the team and pass on his experience to other players.'

And when Martínez named his team for the first game against Liechtenstein, Cristiano was there in the starting line-up, wearing the Number 7 shirt and the captain's armband.

Phew, he was still Portugal's first-choice striker! It had been a difficult few months, what with the World Cup and then his move from Manchester United to Saudi Arabian club Al Nassr, but Cristiano was looking forward to kicking off an exciting new era for his country.

There was also another reason for his excitement – this would be his 197th match for Portugal, making him the number one most-capped male international footballer EVER! So, could he make history in style, with a massive performance?

While João Cancelo scored Portugal's first, and Bernardo scored their second, Cristiano snuck in to grab goals three and four: a penalty, followed by a powerful swerving free kick that flew straight past the poor Liechtenstein keeper.

Goooooooooooooooooooaaaaaaaaaaaaaaaaallllllllllllll llllllllllll!!!!!!!!!!!!!!!!!!!!

Cristiano celebrated in front of the fans with a classic 'Siuuuu!' It felt great to be back scoring for his country, and breaking yet another world record was a lovely bonus.

After that promising start, Martínez's Portugal were even more lethal away against Luxembourg three days later. Cristiano gave his team the lead with an early tap-in, and after that the goals kept coming: one for João Félix, one for Bernardo, another for Cristiano, one for Otávio, and one for Rafael. 6–0!

Yes, Portugal were far from a one-man team these days, but Cristiano was having so much fun that he didn't even mind being subbed off in the sixty-fifth minute for Gonçalo.

'2 games 2 WINS!' he posted on social media

afterwards. 'Happy to have contributed to this very positive start of our national team. Vamos!'

Thrashing teams like Liechtenstein and Luxembourg was a great confidence boost for the new Portugal, but there would be tougher tests ahead against better teams. Could they carry on their winning form? Yes!

Portugal played brilliantly against Bosnia-Herzegovina, and it was Bruno's turn to be the star of the show. After setting up the first goal for Bernardo, he then scored two of his own. 3–0!

For Cristiano, it was a rare international game without a goal, but his droughts never lasted long. Three days later, with Portugal heading for a disappointing 0–0 draw against Iceland, their captain stepped up to save the day, just like he had so many times before. In the eighty-ninth minute, Gonçalo Inácio headed the ball down in the box and there was Cristiano, alert as ever, to put it in the net.

Goooooooooooooooooooaaaaaaaaaaaaaaaallllllllllllll llllllllllll!!!!!!!!!!!!!!!!!!!

But wait – the linesman's flag was up for offside!

'What? No, no, no!' Cristiano told the referee,

wagging his finger. He was confident that he and Gonçalo had both been onside, but what would the VAR review decide?...

Goooooooooooooooooooaaaaaaaaaaaaaaaaaallllllllllllll llllllllllll!!!!!!!!!!!!!!!!!!!

'Yesssssssss!' Cristiano yelled as a big smile spread across his face. Throwing his arms out wide, he ran towards the corner flag, and then turned and called his teammates over to join him. Coming, Captain! Soon, he was in the middle of a big group hug involving every player, including the goalkeeper. What a perfect way to celebrate his 200th cap for Portugal!

'For me it's an unbelievable achievement, it's amazing,' he said after the match. 'And, of course to score the winning goal, it's even more special.'

Four wins out of four – Portugal were flying, and Cristiano's goal of qualifying for Euro 2024 goal was getting closer and closer.

PART 3

EURO 2024
– WE'RE IN!

'Too old', 'past it', 'finished' – those were just some of the things that people had said about him, but Cristiano loved proving his critics wrong. Why should he stop? Even at the age of thirty-eight, he was still enjoying his football, and he was still starring for club and country.

In August 2023, Cristiano led Al-Nassr to glory at the Arab Club Champions Cup. Every time his team needed a hero, he somehow found a way to save the day:

An equaliser against Zamalek to get them through the group stage…

The opening goal in the quarter-finals against Raja

CA...

The only goal in the semi-finals against Al-Shorta...

And like all big-game players, Cristiano saved his best performance until last. With twenty minutes to go in the grand final against Al-Hilal, it didn't look good for Al-Nassr. Not only were they losing 1–0, but they were also down to ten men.

'Come on, CR7 – we need you!' the supporters shouted. 'Do something!'

Cristiano was trying, and he kept trying, even after a painful arm in the face from defender Kalidou Koulibaly. All he needed was one good chance...

In the seventy-third minute, Sultan Al-Ghannam made a bursting run up the right wing, and delivered a dangerous cross into the middle, where Cristiano was waiting, a couple of yards ahead of Koulibaly. With a flick of his right foot, he lifted the ball past the Al-Hilal keeper – 1–1!

Gooooooooooooooooooooaaaaaaaaaaaaaaaalllllllllllllll llllllllllll!!!!!!!!!!!!!!!!!!!!

Game on! 'Let's goooooooo!' Cristiano cried out as he ran back for the restart. Now, Al-Nasr needed to go for the winner...

Cristiano had a goal ruled out for offside and then a shot cleared off the line, but nothing was going to stop him from lifting the trophy. In extra time, Seko Fofana's shot struck the crossbar and bounced back out, and there was Cristiano, alert as ever, to score with a diving header. 2–1!

Goooooooooooooooooooooaaaaaaaaaaaaaaaaallllllllllllll llllllllllll!!!!!!!!!!!!!!!!!!!!

'Yessssss!' Cristiano cheered as his teammates threw their arms around him. Thanks to him, they were about to win the Arab Club Champions Cup!

When the final whistle was eventually blown, the celebrations were even bigger. All the Al-Nassr players and coaches bounced up and down together on the pitch, and Captain Cristiano was at the centre of everything, enjoying every moment.

'Extremely proud to help the team win this important trophy for the first time!' he wrote on social media, next to a picture of him holding the beautiful gold prize.

With club success achieved, Cristiano switched his

focus back to his country. Although Portugal were top of Group J with a perfect record, they weren't on their way to Euro 2024 just yet. They still had work to do and matches to win, starting with an away trip to Slovakia, the team in second place.

Ooof, this one wasn't going to be so easy. Although they didn't have many famous superstars, Slovakia were a very well-organised side who hardly ever lost at home. To beat them, Portugal would have to be at their best in both attack and defence…

In the sixteenth minute, Slovakia's centre-back Denis Vavro thought he had lots of time on the ball, but all of a sudden, he was surrounded by Bruno… and Cristiano! He stole possession and passed the ball to Bruno, but his strike flew straight at the keeper.

'Noooooooo!' Cristiano groaned, throwing his hands to his head in disappointment. What a good chance wasted!

Just before half-time, however, Bruno went for a much harder shot, and scored. 1–0!

'That's more like it!' Cristiano said with a smile, high-fiving his teammate.

Portugal were ahead, but could they hold on to their lead? So far, they hadn't conceded a single goal in qualification, and they weren't going to let that slip now. Diogo Costa kept out any shots that came his way, and everyone else worked hard making blocks, tackles and interceptions, even the forwards. It was a real team effort from Portugal, and eventually they got their reward.

'Very important win in a tough game!' Cristiano said afterwards. 'We remain undefeated!'

With five wins out of five, Portugal were nearly there now.

Cristiano had to miss the next match against Luxembourg for collecting too many yellow cards, but his teammates did a great job without him. Gonçalo Inácio scored two, and so did Gonçalo Ramos and Diogo Jota, with Ricardo Horta, Bruno and João Félix adding one goal each. 9–0!

Six wins out of six! Euro 2024 was now just three points away for Portugal – could they pick them up at home against Slovakia?

Cristiano was back for the big game, and this

time, he wasn't playing as the only central striker; he had Gonçalo Ramos alongside him. Two up front, plus Bruno, Rafael and Bernardo just behind – wow, Portugal were going all-out attack! So, would Martínez's new 4–1–3–2 formation be a success or a failure?

In the eighteenth minute, Bruno chipped a cross into the middle and Gonçalo headed home. 1–0!

Then, ten minutes later, it was Cristiano's turn. When Rafael's cross hit a defender on the arm, he stepped up to score from the penalty spot. 2–0!

Vamoooooooooooos! On a wet night in Porto, Portugal were on fire. They looked like they might score every time they attacked, but their third goal didn't end up coming until the seventy-second minute. It was worth the wait, though.

The move started with midfielder João Palhinha,

Who passed the ball back to Bernardo,

Who played it forward to sub João Félix,

Who gave it to Gonçalo,

Who spread the ball wide to João Cancelo,

Who poked it down the line to Bruno,

Who whipped the ball across the six-yard box,
Where Cristiano was waiting for the tap-in. 3–1!

Gooooooooooooooooooooaaaaaaaaaaaaaaaaalllllllllllllll llllllllllll!!!!!!!!!!!!!!!!!!!!

It was a goal that summed up the new Portugal perfectly – more passing, more attacking, and more working together. As he ran towards the corner flag to do his 'Siuuuu!' celebration, Cristiano turned to point a hand of thanks at Bruno. It was a real pleasure to play with such talented and creative teammates.

Soon, the game was over, and Cristiano could share Portugal's great news with the world:

'Euro 2024 – we're in!'

PART 4

PORTUGAL'S PERFECT TEN

What would Portugal do now? They still had
three Euro qualifiers left to play, so was it time to
experiment and give some new, young players a go?
Not at all – Martínez decided to stick with the same
team because they still had two more ambitious goals
to achieve:

1) Finishing top of the group, which would make
them one of the top seeds for the tournament in
Germany,

2) Finishing with a perfect record – ten wins out of
ten!

Only eight teams had ever done that in Euro
qualification, and Martínez wanted his side to be the

ninth, and the first from Portugal.

Both challenges accepted! Cristiano and his teammates achieved the first of their goals almost immediately, as they battered Bosnia. Even away from home, Martínez still went with an attacking 4–1–3–2 formation, and as a result, Portugal ran riot in the first half.

Cristiano scored a spot-kick to reach eight goals for the campaign. 1–0!

Then he made it nine with a cheeky chip over the keeper. 2–0!

Five minutes later, Bruno blasted home after beautiful long pass from Gonçalo Inácio. 3–0!

Soon after that, João Cancelo curled a shot in from the edge of the box. 4–0!

And finally João Félix poked the ball in from near the penalty spot. 5–0!

Wow, it wasn't even half-time yet! Portugal were making the road to the Euros look so easy.

'Another win and great play by the whole team!' Cristiano declared happily. 'First place in the group guaranteed!'

Right, Portugal needed just two more wins to reach the perfect 10. First up: Liechtenstein away.

After a goalless first half, it was Cristiano who made the breakthrough yet again. Early in the second, he raced on to a pass from Diogo Jota, shrugged off a defender, and fired a powerful shot past the keeper.

Goooooooooooooooooooooaaaaaaaaaaaaaaaaallllllllllllllll llllllllllll!!!!!!!!!!!!!!!!!!!!

With an arm around Diogo, Cristiano looked over at his manager and punched the air with passion. Their dream was still alive!

Ten minutes later, João Cancelo dribbled around the keeper and curled the ball into an empty net. 2–0 – job done, another match won!

Now the last team standing between Portugal and a perfect record was Iceland. Back at Euro 2016, the two teams had drawn 1–1, but a lot had changed since then. For Iceland, that tournament had turned out to be the peak, but for Portugal, it felt like another exciting new era was just beginning. Could they cap off an incredible Euro qualification campaign with one last victory?

Cristiano thought he was about to score in only the second minute of the match. When Bruno's cross curled towards him, he followed the flight carefully and then powered his head towards it... but at the last second, a defender hooked the ball away. So close! Oh well, there was still plenty of time...

But when Otávio hit the post, and then João Félix hit the side netting, some began to wonder if maybe it was Portugal's unlucky day. Not Cristiano, though. He always believed in himself, and in his national teammates too. This time, it was Bruno who got the breakthrough, with a swerving, low strike that skidded into the bottom corner.

'Yessssss!' Cristiano cheered as he watched it go in, waving his right arm in the air. Portugal were nearly there now, but another goal would help make sure...

In the sixty-fifth minute, the Iceland keeper spilled a shot from João Félix, and the ball rolled out towards Cristiano. This was it; his best chance of the game. But before he could get his shot away, the keeper got back up to block it. *Noooooo!* Never mind, the second rebound fell to Ricardo, who grabbed the second goal instead.

Oh well, different scorer, same scoreline – Cristiano wasn't going to get angry over something so silly. Instead, he smiled and gave his teammate a high-five and a hug. The main thing was that Portugal were winning.

Soon, their road to the Euros was over, successfully, and what a campaign it had been: thirty-six goals scored, and only two goals conceded; ten games played, and all ten games won. Yesssss, they had done it!

'100% victorious!' Cristiano wrote on social media. 'Congratulations Portugal!'

But even as he celebrated the historic achievement with his teammates, the doubters had some concerns about him. All it took was one international game without a goal and his critics were back, asking the same old questions:

Was Cristiano the wrong man to lead Portugal at Euro 2024?

Was he holding the team back?

Were they better off without him?

Had he lost his edge at the highest level?

The answer in each case was 'NO!'

Not according to the numbers – with ten goals, he had finished as the second top scorer in the whole of Euro qualifying, ahead of Kylian Mbappé and Harry Kane. And not according to his manager, Martínez, either – 'Cristiano Ronaldo is as hungry as an eighteen-year-old player,' he announced after the match.

Thanks, Boss! But after so many years in the football spotlight, Cristiano wasn't going to let a few negative words affect him. 'Portugal qualified because they played well, they have an excellent team, an excellent coach, and we deserved to go through,' was all he said.

Besides, Cristiano was already looking ahead to the main event itself: Euro 2024. After playing so well to reach the tournament, could Portugal go all the way and actually win it? Their captain was feeling as confident as ever, and he was hoping to prove a few people wrong along the way.

VIRGIL
VAN DIJK

PART 1

A WORLD CUP LEADER AT LAST

20 November 2022

'It's time.'

That's all Virgil wrote in his message on social media, but his millions of followers knew exactly what he was talking about: the 2022 World Cup, of course!

Virgil had been dreaming about this moment since he was a little boy growing up in Breda, and he had been waiting for that dream to come true ever since he made his senior debut for the Netherlands, way back in 2015.

In 2018, the Netherlands had failed to qualify for the tournament in Russia, but this time they would be there in Qatar, and Virgil would be their captain, a World Cup leader at last. No wonder he was so excited!

But when he led his team out onto the pitch for their opening group game against Senegal, Virgil looked as calm and composed as ever. He was born for this – the biggest stage in football.

'Let's goooooooo!' Virgil clapped and cheered before kick-off, and his talking continued all game long.

'Denzel, you've got to close him down quicker!'

'Ref, he's offside!'

'Push up, we're too deep!'

Virgil loved organising everyone around him, but he also loved doing lots of defending too! He bravely blocked a shot from Ismaïla Sarr with his head, and then another from Idrissa Gueye with his legs.

'Come on, go, go, go!'

With Nathan Aké and Matthijs de Ligt alongside Virgil, the Dutch had one of the best defences in the World Cup, but so far, they were struggling to get going in attack. Right wing-back Denzel Dumfries looked dangerous every time he burst forward, but other than that, the Netherlands weren't creating enough chances to win the game.

Could their captain save the day in attack, as well as in defence? Early in the second half, Cody Gakpo swung a corner into the crowded box and Virgil jumped the highest, but he couldn't quite keep his header from flying over the bar.

'Arggggh!' Virgil groaned, clapping his hands in frustration. So close to a first World Cup goal!

In the sixty-second minute, the Dutch manager Louis van Gaal took off Vincent Janssen, and brought on Memphis Depay. But he couldn't make the difference, and more changes were needed, so off came Steven Bergwijn and Steven Berghuis, and on came Davy Klaassen and Teun Koopmeiners.

'Keep going – the goal is coming!' Virgil told his teammates confidently, and he was right. Just when it looked like they'd never score, the Netherlands took the lead. From wide on the left, Frenkie de Jong chipped a curling cross into the box, and in raced Cody to beat the Senegal keeper to the ball. 1–0!

'Yesssss!' Virgil shouted joyfully as he ran from the

halfway line to the corner flag to join in the Dutch celebrations. Hurray, at last they were winning, and in the final minute, Davy scored a second to secure the victory.

'Up and running...' Virgil posted, with a picture of pure relief.

In their second game against Ecuador, the Netherlands had to settle for a 1–1 draw, but their captain wasn't worried at all. Virgil knew that every point was valuable, and they now had four of them, with one last game against Qatar to go. If they won that, they would top the group and go through to the World Cup Round of 16.

'Let's goooooooooooo!'

Cody finished off a fantastic team move midway through the first half, and then early in the second, Frenkie made it 2–0 with a sliding tap-in. Job done! When the final whistle blew, Virgil threw his head back and punched the air.

'Great work, team – on we gooooo!'

Next up for the Netherlands: the USA. After an early scare, the Dutch defence calmed things down and passed the ball around brilliantly, from side to side.

Virgil to Frenkie, Frenkie back to Virgil, Virgil to Denzel, Denzel to Jurrien Timber, Jurrien to Frenkie, Frenkie to Virgil, Virgil to Nathan...

After frustrating the American attackers with their slow, patient passing, suddenly the Dutch moved the ball forward with more speed.

Daley Blind to Memphis, to Marten de Roon, to Davy, to Memphis, to Cody, and then back to Denzel...

He was flying forward up the right wing now, and he spotted Memphis making a great run through the middle. PING! Denzel's pass was perfect, and so was the finish from Memphis. 1–0!

Whoa – what a wonderful team goal! In the build-up, the Netherlands had made twenty-one successful passes in a row, and every player had been involved, including their keeper Andries Noppert.

'Even Johan Cruyff would have been proud of that one!' Virgil joked.

Now, could the Netherlands keep going and get another goal? Yes, just before half-time, Denzel did it again. After bursting up the right wing, he delivered a great cross into the box, where Daley was waiting this time. 2–0!

And the game wasn't over. In the second half, the Dutch still had defending to do. First, Cody cleared a shot off the line, and then so did Denzel.

'Come on, CONCENTRATE!' Virgil called out to his teammates, but a minute later, the USA scored with a fluky flick from Haji Wright. Game ON!

Fortunately, the Netherlands had their captain there to keep them calm and composed for the final twenty minutes. Instead of conceding another goal, they actually scored one of their own, with Denzel racing in at the back post to volley the ball in. 3–1!

Now, it really was game over – the Netherlands were continuing their World Cup journey! Virgil wasn't getting carried away, though; instead, he was taking things step by step.

'Progress,' he wrote to his fans. 'Next up, Quarter-finals.' And a meeting with Lionel Messi! Ooooooh, what a battle that was going to be…

Virgil, however, wasn't focusing on their one vs one:

'It is not me against him, or the Netherlands against him, but the Netherlands against Argentina. No-one can do it on his own, we will have to come up with a good plan.'

So, by working together, could the strong Dutch defence successfully stop Messi? Virgil used his strength and speed to keep him as quiet as possible, but sometimes the Little Magician was simply unstoppable. In the thirty-fifth minute, he set up Argentina's first goal with a magnificent pass that flew through Nathan's legs, and then in the seventy-third minute, he scored their second himself from the penalty spot.

Uh-oh, were the Netherlands about to be knocked out of the World Cup? Not without a fight, no!

'Come on, keep going – it's not over yet!' Virgil encouraged his teammates.

It was time for the Dutch to use their not-so-secret weapon: tall striker Wout Weghorst. He came on in the seventy-eighth minute and changed the game almost immediately.

First, he got a flick on Steven Berghuis's free kick

and it flew into the bottom corner. 2–1!

And then in the last seconds, he scored again, from Teun's seriously clever free kick. 2–2!

'YESSSSSSSSSSSSSS!' Virgil screamed. The Dutch captain wasn't calm and composed anymore; he was fired up and ready to fight on, through extra time, and all the way to... PENALTIES!

For his club, Liverpool, Virgil had only ever taken one spot-kick, in the 2022 EFL Cup final against Chelsea, and he'd scored it in style. So, would he step up now as the captain of his country in the World Cup quarter-finals? Of course! In fact, he even offered to go first.

After placing the ball down on the spot, Virgil took a couple of steps back and then a big, deep breath. Then he ran up and blasted it towards the bottom corner... but the Argentina keeper guessed the right way. SAVED!

Noooooooooooo! Virgil couldn't believe it! With his head bowed, he made the long walk back to the halfway line, wincing at the memory of what he'd just done. Oh well, all he could do now was hope that he wouldn't be the only one who missed...

As it turned out, Virgil wasn't the only one; Enzo Fernández also missed for Argentina, but sadly, so did Steven Berghuis for the Netherlands. So as Lautaro Martínez stepped up, he had the chance to win the shoot-out and... he scored.

NOOOOOOOOOOO! For the Dutch players, it was a devastating moment – losing on penalties was such a painful way to go out of any tournament, but especially the World Cup. As he stood there, staring up at the sky, Virgil couldn't help thinking back to his own spot-kick. If only he'd put his strike slightly further to the left – he would have scored! But it was no use thinking like that. It was over, and the Netherlands were heading home.

'Nothing but proud of this team,' Virgil said a few days later, once the disappointment had started to fade a little. 'We gave it our all but unfortunately it wasn't our tournament.'

What about Euro 2024 – could that be their tournament...?

PART 2

A TOUGH START TO 2023

When the Netherlands kicked off their Euro qualification in March 2023, it felt like a fresh start in some ways. The team had a different manager now, Ronald Koeman, and a new tournament to work towards together. But in other ways, it brought back bad old memories.

When they failed to qualify for the 2018 World Cup, the Netherlands had finished third behind Sweden and France. And who were the other top nation in their Euro 2024 qualifying group now? France! Noooo, not again! Not only that, but the Dutch were starting their campaign with the most difficult match of all — an away trip to Paris. Back in 2017, the Netherlands had lost 4–0 at the Stade de France. This time, they lost 4–0 again!

Under new captain Kylian Mbappé, Les Bleus started brilliantly, and they were 3–0 up within twenty-one minutes. The Dutch, meanwhile, looked slow and disorganised all over the pitch, but especially in defence.

'Arggggh, we've ALL got to hold our line together, otherwise we're playing them onside!' Virgil yelled, blasting the ball into the net in anger.

The Netherlands did improve in the second half, but a 4–0 defeat was still a tough one to take. After the game, Virgil didn't hold back when the journalists asked him questions. 'I don't know if it's the worst international match I've had, but it sure is a big hit,' he admitted honestly. 'We tried to recover after that bad start, but we didn't succeed. We had way too many ball losses and were too weak in the duels.'

Oh well, at least the Netherlands' next game was against Gibraltar at home...

Midway through the first half, Memphis headed home from Denzel's cross. 1–0!

Early in the second half, Nathan went forward and nodded the ball in. 2–0!

And late on, Nathan scored again, with a left-foot shot from the edge of the box. 3–0!

'Hey, maybe we should move you up front!' Virgil joked, high-fiving his fellow defender. He was a happier captain now. Three goals, three points and a clean sheet – that was more like it! After that awful start against France, the Netherlands were now up and running on the road to Euro 2024.

But before their next set of qualifiers in September, Virgil and his teammates had a different international trophy to try and win: the UEFA Nations League.

Back in 2019, the Netherlands had lost to Portugal in the first-ever Nations League final. They hoped to do better this time, but even with home crowds cheering them on, unfortunately they failed to even reach the final. There was initial promise; they went 1–0 up in their semi-final against Croatia, thanks to a goal from Donyell Malen, but after that, things fell apart, and they ended up losing 4–2 in extra time.

'Come onnnnn, you can't just let him turn and

shoot like that!' Virgil screamed while Croatia were celebrating their crucial third goal. Weak defending, sloppy passes, poor tackles in the penalty area – his team was making waaaay too many silly mistakes!

Unfortunately, the dodgy Netherlands defending continued in their next match, the third place play-off against Italy.

Three times they failed to clear the ball out of their own box, until eventually Federico Dimarco scored. 1–0!

'Offside!' the Dutch defence cried when Davide Frattesi fired a shot past the keeper, but no – after a long VAR review, it turned out they were wrong. 2–0!

When it came to one on ones, Virgil was usually the best defender around, but this time, he was fooled by Federico Chiesa, who just shifted the ball onto his weaker left foot and scored. 3–1!

Booooooooooooooooooooooooo! Oh dear, the Dutch fans weren't happy at all.

Four games played, three games lost, only one game won – it had been a really tough start to 2023 for the team, but Virgil was determined to turn things around.

After a much-needed summer break, the Netherlands would come bouncing back stronger than ever, and qualify for the Euros in style. Their captain was confident about that.

PART 3

BOUNCING BACK WITH A BOOM!

As Virgil led the Netherlands team out onto the pitch in Eindhoven, their opponents Greece were sitting three points ahead of them in Euro 2024 Qualifying Group B. The table would hopefully look a lot different after the final whistle, though.

'Let's gooooooooooooooo!'

Right from kick-off, the Netherlands played like a team with a point to prove. In the sixteenth minute, Denzel headed down Daley's corner, and Marten blasted the ball into the bottom corner. 1–0!

'Yessssssssss!' Virgil yelled, throwing his arms up in the air. They were bouncing back already, and by half-time, it was already game over for Greece.

First, Cody finished off a flowing team move, involving Denzel and Xavi Simons. 2–0!

Then Denzel delivered an excellent cross to Wout, for a header he couldn't miss. 3–0!

Three goals, three points and yes, a clean sheet – the Dutch defence made sure of that. Walking off the pitch, Virgil was a proud captain again. Together, the team was moving in the right direction, towards a place at Euro 2024.

Next up for the Netherlands: Republic of Ireland away, just three days later, but the Dutch team got off to a dreadful start in Dublin. In only the second minute, Virgil jumped for a header in his own box, and the ball struck him on the arm.

'Handball, penalty!' screamed every Ireland player, and the referee pointed to the spot. Up stepped Adam Idah, who sent the keeper the wrong way. 1–0!

The Netherlands were behind, but there was no need for their players to panic. Grabbing the ball out of the net, Virgil calmly led his team forward, ready for the restart. Of course they could fight back – the game had only just begun!

Fifteen minutes later, the Netherlands were level. Cody dribbled forward from deep and slid a perfect pass through to Denzel, who was fouled by the outrushing keeper. Another penalty! Cody took it, blasting the ball into the bottom corner. 1–1!

Now, for another goal to win the game...

Donyell shot straight at the keeper twice,

Xavi's strike swerved up and over the bar...

...But finally, the Netherlands got the goal they needed. Frenkie spotted Denzel on the run from right to left, and he had the skill to deliver the perfect lofted pass. When it arrived, Denzel chested the ball down to Wout, who guided it past the keeper. 2–1!

Phew! Virgil was a mightily relieved man. At last, the Netherlands were ahead; now, he had some serious defending to do...

Chiedozie Ogbene tried to turn him in the box, but the Dutch captain stood strong. Moments later, Ogbene crossed the ball into the middle, but again Virgil was there to make the clearance.

In the ninety-first minute, Ryan Manning curled in one last corner, but Virgil headed the ball far away from danger.

When he heard the final whistle blow at last, Virgil threw his head back and roared – comeback complete! 'After a tricky start, we found a way to win…' he wrote on social media. 'That's all that matters.'

Besides, the Netherlands had an even bigger match to think about next: France at home. The team had certainly made progress since the 4–0 defeat in Paris, but could they prove it on the pitch against Mbappé and co?

Although the game still ended in defeat for the Dutch, it was 2–1 to France rather than 4–0, and it could have been even better if they'd taken their chances. Joey Veerman, Xavi, Donyell – they all could and should have scored, long before Quilindschy Hartman's late goal. But ultimately, their defence had been undone by two moments of Mbappé magic.

Never mind, the Netherlands knew what they now needed to do to reach Euro 2024: win all three of their last group games, starting with Greece away…

'Let's goooooooooooooooo!'

With the score still 0–0, Virgil went forward for a

corner midway through the first half and managed
to cause complete chaos. As the cross came into the
box, a Greek defender fell to the floor and dragged the
Dutch captain down too, while also tripping up one
of his own teammates, who then crashed into their
goalkeeper! It all ended with a pile of players down on
the grass, and poor Virgil was at the bottom of it.

'Hey!' he managed to shout out, while holding his
hurt face. Surely, that had to be a penalty? Yes, the
referee pointed to the spot, and up stepped Wout...
but the keeper dived down and saved it!

Oh well, it was a setback, but there was no need for
the Dutch players to panic. 'Keep going, the goal will
come!' Virgil urged his teammates on.

But in the second half, the Netherlands missed
chance after chance, and the minutes ticked by
without a winning goal. Oh dear, a draw would be a
disaster...

With seconds to go, substitute Brian Brobbey
controlled the ball just inside the Greece box and then
slipped a pass through for Denzel, who was fouled as
he ran to reach it.

'PENALTY!' screamed every Dutch player, coach and supporter.

The referee gave it, but now the big question was: who was going to take it?

Would Wout try again, after missing the first time? No. Okay, well, what about Steven Bergwijn, or Donyell, or Denzel? In fact, it was the captain himself who walked forward. Wow, what a moment! This was Virgil's chance to put things right, after his penalty pain in the World Cup against Argentina.

As he placed the ball down, someone pointed a green laser at his face, but Virgil was so focused that he hardly seemed to notice. When the whistle blew, he took a big, deep breath and then ran up and... sent the keeper the wrong way! 1–0!

Goooooooooooooooooooooaaaaaaaaaaaaaaaalllllllllllllll llllllllllll!!!!!!!!!!!!!!!!!!

Yesssss, Virgil had done it; he was the Dutch hero once again! Over by the corner flag, he jumped up and punched the air with a 'Boom!!!'

Thanks to their Captain Cool, the Netherlands were nearly on their way to the Euros now...

PART 4

EURO 2024, LET'S GO!

One more win – that was all the Netherlands needed now to reach Euro 2024. They had two games left to get the job done, but wouldn't it be nice to do it straight away, at home against the Republic of Ireland?

'Let's goooooooooooooooo!'

In front of a packed crowd at the Amsterdam Arena, the Dutch team got off to the perfect start. In the tenth minute, Wout used his strength to escape from his marker near the halfway line, and then powered forward, all the way into the box, where he slammed a shot into the roof of the net. 1–0!

'Whoa, what a run that was!' Virgil cheered when he finally caught up with his tall teammate. Surely, the

Netherlands were nearly there now?

Somehow, despite having nineteen shots, the Dutch failed to score a second goal, but luckily that one turned out to be enough. When the final whistle blew, Virgil punched the air with both fists and smiled up at the sky. It had always been an easy journey, but in the end, the Netherlands had achieved their aim:

'EURO 2024, Here we come!'

Suddenly, the stands of the Amsterdam Arena were a sea of orange, with confetti and streamers as well as shirts and flags. Down on the pitch, the Dutch players hugged and high-fived each other, and then did a lap of honour to thank the fans for their support.

'EURO 2024, Let's gooooo!'

The celebrations carried on late into the night, and they continued in the Netherlands' next match too, three days later against Gibraltar. With Euro qualification secured, their players could relax and attack with more freedom and flair, letting the passing football flow.

Joey dribbled through and set up Calvin Stengs for his first international goal. 1–0!

Midfielder Mats Wieffer powered in a brilliant header. 2–0!

Teun poked Quilindschy's cross past the keeper. 3–0!

Calvin played a one-two with Donyell and scored again. 4–0!

Calvin curled the ball into the top corner to complete his hat-trick. 5–0!

And finally, Cody came on and scored within seconds. 6–0!

In defence, Virgil hardly had anything to do all game, but it was good to see the Dutch forwards having so much fun together. Cody, Xavi, Donyell, Calvin, Brian, Noa Lang – these talented youngsters were the future of the Netherlands national team, and it looked pretty bright from where their captain was standing, at centre-back!

Were they ready to shine consistently in match after match at a major international tournament? It was hard to know, but it would be exciting to find out. Eeeek – Virgil couldn't wait for the Euros to start! It was going to be all the more special for him because

it would be his first, having missed the Euro 2020
tournament with an ACL injury.

Would the Netherlands be one of the favourites
to win Euro 2024, along with France and Germany?
No, probably not, but with their blend of youth
and experience, speed and skill, power and passing,
aggression and calm, at their best, they were capable
of beating anyone.

LUKA MODRIĆ

PART 1

WORLD CUP MEDALLISTS ONCE AGAIN

November 2022

In 2018, Croatia had reached the World Cup final in Russia. Four years on, they were about to compete in football's greatest international tournament once again. So, could they carry on their successful run in Qatar?

'We are ready!' said Luka, their leader and superstar Number 10.

At thirty-seven years old, this would be Luca's fourth and probably final World Cup, but the Croatia captain wasn't showing any signs of slowing down. He had made forty-five appearances for his club, Real Madrid, during the 2021–22 season, helping them win the Spanish League title and the UEFA Champions League trophy. For his country, meanwhile, he had hardly ever missed a match, and he never had a bad game. He was Mr Reliable at the heart of the midfield, using his skill and experience to keep the team ticking along towards victory.

Luka had led Croatia to the 2022 World Cup without much trouble, but now getting them through the group stage of the tournament was going to be a more difficult task. Not only were they up against Belgium, the Number 2-ranked team in the world, but they would also have to take on two of the most-improved sides in international football, Morocco and Canada.

'Let's gooooo!' Luka called out as Croatia kicked things off against Morocco. Although some of his teammates from 2018 had now retired, they still had Dejan Lovren in defence, Ivan Perišić and Andrej Kramarić in attack, and alongside Luka in the middle, Marcelo Brozović and Mateo Kovačić. Together, the three of them formed one of the most-feared midfields in the whole of international football.

As hard as they tried, however, Croatia just could not find a way past Morocco. Ivan's long-range strike swerved just over the crossbar, Nikola Vlašić's shot rolled straight at the keeper, and Luka's left-foot blast flew high over the bar too.

'Noooooooooo!' he gasped, covering his face with his hands. A 0–0 draw was a disappointing start to the tournament for Croatia, but their captain wasn't feeling too worried yet. The good news was that the team already had a point and a clean sheet, and they still had two group games to go.

Against Canada, however, Croatia found themselves 1–0 down after only two minutes. Uh-oh, time to panic? No, instead the shock seemed to wake their players up. As the game went on, they got better and better until eventually the equaliser arrived. Mateo passed to Ivan, who slipped a brilliant ball through for Andrej to score. 1–1!

'Yesssssssss!' Luka cheered, punching the air with both fists. 'That's more like it!'

After that, Croatia cruised to victory, with goals

from Marko Livaja, Andrej and Lovro Majer. It was so comfortable that Luka even got a five-minute rest at the end!

He was back for the next match, though: the big one against Belgium. While Croatia only needed a draw to go through, their opponents now needed a win after a surprise defeat to Morocco. It was all set up to be an absolute cracker...

For the first sixty minutes, it was a pretty even game, but after that, it was mostly Belgium pushing forward on the attack and Croatia just about holding on at the back. First Romelu Lukaku hit the post, then he headed over, and finally he chested the ball straight at the keeper in the six-yard box.

'Phew!' Luka sighed with relief, watching with his hands on his head. Somehow, Belgium didn't score a winning goal, and so when the final whistle blew, Croatia were the lucky ones going through.

'Proud of this team and happy to be in the next round,' Luka said afterwards. 'We keep going!!!'

Next up, in the Last 16: Japan. The 'Samurai Blue' had already surprised Germany and Spain in the group stage – but could they now do the same to Croatia? The answer was… nearly. Japan did take the lead late in the first half, but they stayed strong and fought back early in the second, thanks to a stunning header from Ivan. 1–1!

Now, could Croatia go on and win it? A few minutes later, Luka chested the ball down on the edge of the box and hit a shot that dipped and swerved towards the top corner… but the Japan keeper flew through the air to tip it over the bar.

'Ooooooooh!' Luka gasped, jumping up and down first with excitement and then disappointment.

'So close to another moment of Modrić magic!' exclaimed the commentators on TV.

In the end, the winning goal never arrived for either team. It was still 1–1 after ninety minutes, and it was still 1–1 after 120 minutes too. There was only one thing for it: PENALTIES!

By then, Luka had already been taken off, so he had to support his teammates from the sidelines, thinking, 'Please don't let this be the end of our World Cup journey!' And thanks to their super keeper, Dominik

Livaković, it wasn't. With the pressure on, he saved spot-kicks from Takumi Minamino, Kaoru Mitoma, and Maya Yoshida to send Croatia into the World Cup quarter-finals again.

'Yesssssssssss!' Luka yelled as he raced over to hug their hero keeper. Their World Cup dream was still alive, and next up: Brazil!

Éder Militão, Casemiro, Rodrygo, Vinícius Júnior – Luka knew how dangerous his talented Real Madrid teammates could be, and they had just shown it by thrashing South Korea 4–1 in the Round of 16. Croatia were going to have to be very careful, and play a patient, counterattacking game...

Against the tournament favourites, the whole team performed brilliantly. Dominik made super saves in goal, Dejan and Joško Gvardiol were big and brave in defence, and Croatia's captain and midfield maestro? Magnificent – Luka showed just what a big-game player he was. Every touch, and every movement, was so effective and intelligent.

With a clever drop of his shoulder, he glided away from Fred,

He raced in to steal the ball off Casemiro and then curled a teasing cross towards the back post,

Faced with two defenders, he twisted and turned until one of them fouled him,

He looked up and delivered a long diagonal ball which landed right on Ivan's boot,

And again and again, he dribbled out of tight spaces to lead Croatia forward on the attack.

Even at thirty-seven, Luka was still as energetic as ever, and with the game still tied at 0–0 after ninety minutes, there was no way he was coming off this time. What if this was it – his last-ever World Cup match?

In the 105th minute, that looked likely. With two beautiful one-twos, Neymar Jr finally burst his way through the defence, dribbled around Dominik, and fired the ball into the net. 1–0 to Brazil!

Noooooooooooo! Some of the Croatian players fell to the floor in despair, but not Luka. Standing with his hands on his hips, he simply sighed, tucked a strand of hair behind his ear, and then carried on playing. Croatia were the comeback kings and there was still plenty of time to turn things around…

Ten minutes later, Luka led his team forward again with a neat pass to Nikola,

Who played it up the left wing to Mislav Oršić,

Who cut it across the box to Bruno Petković. BANG! His shot deflected off Marquinhos's leg and dropped into the bottom corner. 1–1!

Luka threw his tired arms up in the air, and then jogged over to join the team celebrations. They had done it, they were back in the game, but Croatia hadn't won yet, though. When extra time ended, there was only one thing for it: PENALTIES… AGAIN!

This time, Luka was still on the pitch and able to take part. He went third for his country, after Dominik had already saved from Rodrygo. Now, if their captain could score, Croatia would be so close to a place in the World Cup semi-finals.

After a slow run-up, Luka sent the Brazil keeper the wrong way. GOAL! As he turned away, Croatia's Captain Calm swung his right fist high into the air. 'Come onnnnnnnnnnnnn!' he cried.

Moments later, it was all over and the whole team

was rushing over to celebrate with Dominik. Croatia had done it; they had beaten the might of Brazil!

The next day, once things had calmed down, Luka posted a short message on social media, which summed up both his team and his whole incredible football career:

'Never. Give. Up.'

So, could Croatia keep going and reach a second World Cup final in a row? No, sadly that turned out to be a step too far for Luka's team. In the semi-finals, they were soundly beaten by Lionel Messi's Argentina, who simply had too much energy and power in attack.

Oh well, never mind – Croatia had done so well to reach the semi-finals once again, and their World Cup wasn't over yet. They still had the third-place play-off against... Morocco. Again?! In the group stage, their match had finished 0–0, but what about now, with a Bronze Medal up for grabs? Thankfully, it turned out to be a very different game.

First Croatia pulled off the perfect free kick routine, which ended with Joško scoring a spectacular diving header. 1–0!

Then a minute later, Morocco equalised from another free kick. 1–1!

Wow, two goals, and they hadn't even played ten minutes! After that wild start, the game calmed down and Croatia took control, led by Luka, their little midfield maestro. With half-time approaching, he pushed his team up the pitch with a quick pass to Mateo,

Who laid it off to Marko,

Who played it left to Mislav,

Who curled a shot over the Morocco keeper, and in off the post. 2–1!

'Yessssssss!' Luka yelled, watching from near the halfway line. He himself would finish the tournament with zero goals and zero assists, but he was worth so much more than that to his team. He was their leader, and their heartbeat, at the centre of everything.

Fifty minutes later, that strike turned out to have been the winner. 'YESSSSSSSSS!' the Croatia players cried out while they hugged each other on the pitch. Second place in 2018, and now third place in 2022 – what a successful spell for such a small

European nation!

'World Cup Medallists once again,' Luka wrote in a message to the fans. 'Proud!'

PART 2

SO NEAR IN THE UEFA NATIONS LEAGUE

So, would the 2022 World Cup be the end for Luka in terms of international football? No, he wasn't ready to retire just yet.

'We have confirmed that Croatia have a great team, with a very good future ahead, and we have to continue,' Luka said straight after they won the Bronze Medal against Morocco. 'At the least, I want to continue until the Nations League games and then we will see what happens.'

The Croatia fans were delighted – hurray, their inspirational captain was carrying on for now! They were really going to need Luka's experience and skill in the UEFA Nations League Finals in June 2023, and before that, they also had their first two tricky Euro 2024 qualifiers to play:

1) At home against Wales

Andrej's first-half strike looked like it was going to be the winner, but no, Nathan Broadhead equalised late in injury-time, seconds after Luka had been subbed off.

'Arghhh, we were so close!' he groaned in frustration on the sidelines. It really felt like they'd just thrown away two precious points.

2) Away against Turkey

Three days later, Croatia bounced back with a much better display. Mateo got both goals, and Mario Pašalić got both assists, but Luka was pleased with the whole team performance. This time, they all stayed strong and focused until the final whistle blew, even after their captain had left the field.

'Well done, guys!' Luka clapped proudly. Two games, four points – Croatia were up and running on their road to the Euros. Now, for the Nations League Finals…

First up, in the semi-finals, they faced the

Netherlands. Beating the Dutch was going to be difficult, but Croatia's task got even harder when Donyell Malen scored before half-time.

'Come on, why was no-one closing him down?!' Luka called out, waving his arms angrily.

What Croatia needed now was a really strong second-half comeback, and that's what they produced, inspired by their incredible captain.

Give up? No way, Luka didn't know the meaning of those two words. In the fifty-third minute, he rushed in to beat Cody Gakpo to a bouncing ball, and as he panicked in his own box, the Dutch player dragged him down. Penalty!

So, who was going to take it? As he lay on the grass, Luka looked up and pointed at Andrej. Yes, captain! Croatia's striker stepped up and sent the keeper the wrong way. 1–1!

'Now, we go on and win this!' Luka told his teammates as they celebrated together.

Yes, captain! In a crowded box, Luka Ivanušec did brilliantly to pick out Mario, who volleyed the ball in. 2–1!

Hurraaaaaaaay, their comeback was complete… or was it? In the very last minute, the ball bounced dangerously around the Croatia box, until Noa Lang steered it into the net. 2–2!

'Noooooooooo!' Luka yelled, throwing his hands to his head. He didn't let the disappointment last long, though; as quickly as he could, he turned it into determination. Now, he had to find a way for his team to win in extra time…

From wide on the left wing, Luka poked the ball through to Bruno, and then kept running for the one-two. His teammate didn't need him, though. With a beautiful spin, Bruno escaped from his marker and then fired a dipping shot into the bottom corner. 3–2!

'Yessssssssss!' Luka yelled out in triumph.

So, would that goal be enough to send Croatia through to the final? Maybe, but it was best to make sure. When Bruno was fouled in the box, Luka stepped up to the spot and… placed an unstoppable penalty just inside the post. 4–2!

Goooooooooooooooooooooaaaaaaaaaaaaaaaalllllllllllllll llllllllllll!!!!!!!!!!!!!!!!!!!!

Luka ran towards the corner flag and then jumped into the arms of the waiting subs. What a feeling – Croatia were through to the Nations League Final!

And there, they would face… Spain, who had beaten Italy 2–1 in the other semi-final. Bring it on; Luka and his teammates couldn't wait! Second at the 2018 World Cup, third in 2022 – surely, it was Croatia's turn to finish first and lift a trophy at last?

Midway through the first half, Luka floated a beautiful long ball into the box and Ivan headed it down towards the bottom corner…

Was this it, their match-winning moment?

But no – the Spain keeper scrambled across to save it. Nearly!

Unfortunately, that turned out to be Croatia's best chance in the whole 120 minutes. Another 0–0 draw – yet again, one of their games was going to… PENALTIES!

As they huddled together for a quick team-talk, the Croatia players were feeling confident. At the 2022 World Cup, their hero keeper Dominik had helped them beat both Japan and Brazil in shoot-outs, whereas Spain had lost their only one against Morocco without scoring a single spot-kick!

But this time, both teams made a perfect start to the shoot-out. Nikola, Marcelo and Luka all scored for Croatia, and so did Joselu, Rodri and Mikel Merino for Spain. 3–3!

With each successful penalty, the pressure was building in the stadium. Someone had to miss eventually, but who would it be? Lovro went next for Croatia and... the Spain keeper saved it with his legs!

Noooooooooooo!

'Unlucky Lovro – come on, we can still win this!' Luka clapped and cheered with his teammates on the halfway line. Surely, Spain weren't going to score all five? No, their defender Aymeric Laporte went last, and his shot crashed back off the crossbar.

Phew, Croatia were still in the shoot-out! But it was sudden death now, which meant they couldn't afford to make any more mistakes...

Up stepped Bruno and... he fired the ball too close to the keeper. SAVED!

Noooooooooooo!

Then up stepped Dani Carvajal and… he chipped a Panenka over Dominik as he dived down to his right. GOAL!

NOOOOOOOOOO!

While the Spain players raced around the pitch celebrating, Luka let his head drop and his heart sink. Arghhhhh – football could be so cruel sometimes! He wandered slowly around the pitch in a daze, shaking hands and clapping the supporters, but he kept sighing and shaking his head.

How…? Why…? What if…?

Croatia had got so near to winning the UEFA Nations League Final, but ultimately, it was another international trophy lost, and that was going to hurt for a long, long time.

PART 3

ONE MORE MAJOR TOURNAMENT?

So, would that painful Nations League final be the end for Luka in terms of international football? No, even at the age of thirty-eight, and after 166 appearances for his country, he still wasn't ready to retire just yet!

The Croatia fans breathed a big sigh of relief – phew, their inspirational captain was staying, to lead them to one more major tournament! For all their talented younger players like Joško, Lovro, Luka and Nikola, the team still really needed Luka's experience and skill, especially if they were going to reach Euro 2024.

After their Nations League adventure, Croatia had some catching up to do in Qualification Group D.

Turkey were top with nine points from four matches,

Followed by Armenia with six from three,

Followed by Wales with four from four,

And Croatia with four points from just two matches.

'Let's gooooooo!' Luka urged his teammates on, and they restarted the campaign in style, with a 5–0 thrashing of bottom-placed Latvia.

Although Luka didn't get any goals or assists himself, he was involved in almost every move. A killer first touch, followed by a quick, slick pass, and ZOOM! the team was racing forward on another attack!

That victory took Croatia up to seven points, but they had to keep winning if they were going to overtake Turkey at the top. Next up: Armenia away. The Armenians would sit deep and make things very difficult, but could Croatia find a way through? Yes! In the twelfth minute, Luka's corner bounced down in the crowded box, flicked off a defender's leg, and then landed at Andrej's feet for a tap-in. 1–0!

But hang on, the flag was up for offside, so the final decision would have to be made by VAR. After a long,

anxious wait, the referee blew his whistle and pointed
to the halfway line, which meant…

'GOAL!'

'Yessssssss!' Luka yelled, punching the air with
passion. It certainly wasn't one of the prettiest goals
that Croatia would ever create, but he knew just how
important it might be.

He was right. Despite their captain's best
playmaking efforts, Croatia failed to score again, and
so Andrej's ugly goal-mouth scramble turned out to be
the difference. Oh well, job done – with two wins in
a week, they were now tied at the top of the table on
ten points with Turkey. And their next match was at
home to Turkey…

'Come on, Croatia!' the fans cheered at the sold-out
Opus Arena in Osijek. During the first half, however,
their team was having a total nightmare. The passing
was too slow and sloppy, and the defending was all
over the place. As a result, Turkey looked dangerous
every time they attacked!

In the thirtieth minute, the first goal finally arrived.
As Barış Alper Yılmaz chased after a through-ball,

Dominik made the bad decision to come rushing out of his box. All that did was make it easier for Yılmaz to lift a shot over him and into the net. 1–0!

Uh-oh, Croatia were in real trouble now.

'Come on, wake up – we need to win this!' Luka tried to get his team going again, but with Andrej and Ivan both out injured, they were missing that finishing touch. Mateo had a shot cleared off the line, Marcelo's volley went high and wide, and then Bruno fired the ball straight at the keeper.

But just when time was running out for Croatia, it looked like they'd been given a glorious opportunity. From a corner, the ball appeared to strike the arm of a Turkey defender, and the referee pointed to the penalty spot!

Was it really a handball, though? The VAR told the referee to take a look at the screen, and unfortunately for Croatia, he changed his mind. No penalty! And so after one last weak header from sub striker Dion Beljo, it was all over – Croatia 0 Turkey 1.

Booooooooooooooooooooo!

It was a bad result, but Luka and his teammates had

the chance to put things right three days later, away against Wales. If Croatia could win, they'd move up to thirteen points and their Euro qualification would be back on track. But instead, they slumped to a shocking second straight defeat...

There were warning signs in the first half, but the Croatia defence didn't listen or learn. Then early in the second, the Welsh attackers broke through with ease again. David Brooks flicked the ball on and suddenly Harry Wilson was sprinting away from Domagoj Vida to score past Dominik. 1–0!

Fifteen minutes later, things got even worse for Croatia. Daniel James crossed the ball in from the left and Wilson flicked it into the far corner. 2–0!

'Oh, come onnn!' Luka shouted, throwing his arms up in frustration. What on earth was going on? It was like his team had forgotten how to defend properly! In the seventy-fifth minute, Mario did get one goal back for Croatia, from a curling Luka corner, but Wales held on for a famous win.

Suddenly, the group had been blown wide open, with Croatia, Wales, and even Armenia all now fighting for second place behind Turkey. Croatia had two crucial games left to pull off yet another comeback and qualify automatically for the Euros.

PART 4

EURO 2024, HERE WE GO!

Two games, two wins – for Croatia, the situation was pretty simple when the squad met up in mid-November 2023. The good news was that Andrej was back in attack, and so was Ante Budimir, an experienced striker who played for Spanish club Osasuna.

'Welcome, I hope you brought goals with you!' Luka joked.

And the bad news? Well, actually, there wasn't any, really. Except for poor Ivan, every Croatian player was fit and fired up for their final push towards the Euros.

First up: Latvia away.

Luckily, it didn't take Croatia long to get the

breakthrough. In the fifth minute, Captain Luka whipped a ball into the box and the other Luka – Ivanušec – set up Lovro to score. 1–0!

Phew! Now that their team was winning, the Croatia players relaxed a little and let their best football flow. On the right, Josip Stanišić passed to Captain Luka, who played a one-two with a beautiful backheel.

Olé!

Josip burst forward up the wing, and then fired the ball across to Lovro, who flicked it back for Andrej to shoot. 2–0!

'That's more like it!' Luka cheered while the players shared a big team hug together. Sixteen minutes into the first half, and it was already job done, match won.

'One more step to our goal!' Luka posted on social media afterwards. 'Well done Croatia!'

With one game to go, they were now back in second place, two points ahead of Wales and five ahead of Armenia.

Next up: Armenia at home.

It was a nervy night in Zagreb, for all the Croatia

players, coaches and supporters. A win, and they would be off to the Euros. A defeat, and they would have to fight it out in the play-offs. A draw, and a lot of different things could happen, depending on the scoreline between Wales and Turkey. When the news spread around the stadium that Wales had taken an early lead, it only added to the tense atmosphere.

'Come on, Croatia – now we REALLY need a goal!'

The forwards were doing their best, but it wasn't easy to score against a team like Armenia. They had eight players back protecting their own box, so Croatia had no choice but to patiently pass the ball around and wait for an opportunity to arrive…

With half-time approaching, Luka spread the ball right to Andrej, but then when he got it back, he switched it suddenly left to Borna Sosa. Whoa, Armenia hadn't been expecting that, and it gave Borna the time and space to deliver his best cross, right onto Ante's head. 1–0!

Yessssssss, at last, they were winning! As the team celebrated together, Luka saved his best hugs for the two heroes, Ante and Borna. Now, could Croatia get another goal to make things safe and calm?

Luka's long-range rocket flew straight at the keeper,

Marcelo's swerving strike bounced wide,

Andrej's shot was saved,

And so was another from Marcelo.

Oh well – fortunately 1–0 was enough in the end. Croatia had done it; they had secured second place, and more importantly, their spot at the finals!

After lots of hugs with all his teammates, Luka couldn't wait to share the happy news with his fans across the world: 'Euro 2024. Here we go!'

It hadn't been the easiest of qualification campaigns for Croatia, but the rocky road didn't matter now. What mattered was that the team was on their way to Germany, and soon it would be time for them to do what they did best: play in a major international tournament.

How exciting! And for Luka, would these Euros be the end in terms of international football? Only time would tell, but one thing was for sure: the Croatia captain was going to fight until the final whistle to try and lift the trophy for his country.

ACTIVITIES

TOURNAMENT PLANNER

We've been waiting for this moment for four years, but the 2024 European Championships are finally here! Fill in the tables over the page when all the group games have been played, then continue on with the round of 16, quarter-finals and semi-finals to plot the path to the final!

P	=	Played
W	=	Won
D	=	Drawn
L	=	Lost
F	=	Goals for
A	=	Goals against
PTS	=	Points

GROUP STAGE

GROUP A	P	W	D	L	F	A	PTS
Germany							
Scotland							
Hungary							
Switzerland							

GROUP B	P	W	D	L	F	A	PTS
Spain							
Croatia							
Italy							
Albania							

GROUP C	P	W	D	L	F	A	PTS
Slovenia							
Denmark							
Serbia							
England							

GROUP D	P	W	D	L	F	A	PTS
Play-Off Winner Path A							
Netherlands							
Austria							
France							

GROUP E	P	W	D	L	F	A	PTS
Belgium							
Slovakia							
Romania							
Play-Off Winner Path B							

GROUP F	P	W	D	L	F	A	PTS
Turkey							
Play-Off Winner Path C							
Portugal							
Czechia							

LAST 16

The winner and the runner-up of each
group go through to the Round of 16, plus four of the
best-performing third placed teams.
Fill in the teams and the scores below.

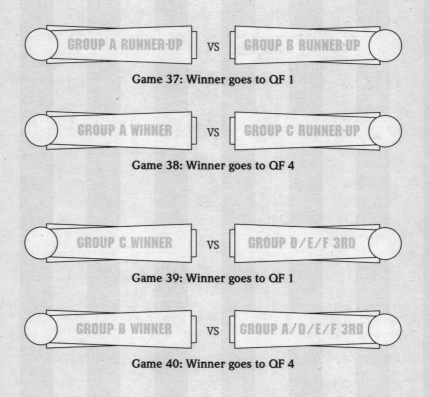

GROUP A RUNNER-UP VS GROUP B RUNNER-UP

Game 37: Winner goes to QF 1

GROUP A WINNER VS GROUP C RUNNER-UP

Game 38: Winner goes to QF 4

GROUP C WINNER VS GROUP D/E/F 3RD

Game 39: Winner goes to QF 1

GROUP B WINNER VS GROUP A/D/E/F 3RD

Game 40: Winner goes to QF 4

GROUP D RUNNER-UP VS GROUP E RUNNER-UP

Game 41: Winner goes to QF 2

GROUP F WINNER VS GROUP A/B/C 3RD

Game 42: Winner goes to QF 2

GROUP D WINNER VS GROUP F RUNNER-UP

Game 43: Winner goes to QF 3

GROUP E WINNER VS GROUP A/B/C/D 3RD

Game 44: Winner goes to QF 3

QUARTER FINALS

Fill in the teams from the previous rounds in the
boxes and add the scores when the game is over.

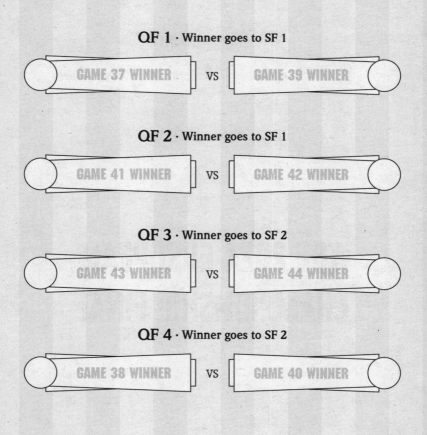

QF 1 · Winner goes to SF 1

GAME 37 WINNER   VS   GAME 39 WINNER

QF 2 · Winner goes to SF 1

GAME 41 WINNER   VS   GAME 42 WINNER

QF 3 · Winner goes to SF 2

GAME 43 WINNER   VS   GAME 44 WINNER

QF 4 · Winner goes to SF 2

GAME 38 WINNER   VS   GAME 40 WINNER

SEMI FINALS

Nearly there – the winners of these go to the
finals, the loser to the third place match.

SF 1 · Winner goes to Final

QF 1 WINNER   VS   QF 2 WINNER

SF 2 · Winner goes to Final

QF 3 WINNER   VS   QF 4 WINNER

THE 2024 EUROPEAN CHAMPIONSHIP FINAL

SF 1 WINNER   VS   SF 2 WINNER

TOURNAMENT SUMMARY CHART

When it's all over, you can fill in all the details.
How did your team do? Did you support a World Cup-
winning team, or is it a case of better luck next time?

Winner	_____
Runner-up	_____
Third place	_____
Fourth place	_____
Golden boot	_____
Goal of the tournament scored by	_____
Best match	_____
Number of goals scored	_____
Number of yellow cards	_____
Number of red cards	_____

DESIGN YOUR OWN SHIRT

Here is your chance to make up your very own shirt.
This could be a special edition for your school team,
the team you support, or your family football team.
Use the space below to draw in the details.
You can have advertising if you like,
to make it look really professional!

DRAW YOUR OWN BADGE

Now you will need your own football team badge
to go on your lovely new shirt. Use the space below
to design it – think about how it will look when it is
small on a shirt – and colour it in when you are done.
Use family or football imagery, or things that
relate to the city or countryside around
you to make it look really special.

FUN FOOTBALL FACTS

EARLY DAYS

The first European Championships were held in France in 1960. Only four nations competed: France, Yugoslavia, the Soviet Union and Czechoslovakia. Three of those nations no longer exist! The Soviet Union defeated Yugoslavia 2–1 in the final.

EARLY DOORS

Russian striker Dmitri Kirichenko scored the fastest goal in a finals tournament when he burst through the Greek defence to score against them only 67 seconds into their 2004 group stage clash. The unfancied Greeks had the last laugh, however, as they went on to stun Portugal in the final and win the trophy.

EVER-PRESENT

Germany (including previous appearances
as West Germany) has never failed to qualify for a
European Championships, and is the tournament's
most successful nation, with more wins, goals and
points than any other team. The only team with a
better goal difference overall is the Netherlands.

NEVER-PRESENT

Norway's failure to qualify
for the 2024 finals extends
their drought to six championships – their last
appearance at any international tournament was at
Euro 2000. Players like Erling Haaland and Martin
Ødegaard face another frustrating summer on the sofa.

GOAL MACHINE

French legend Michel Platini scored nine goals in only five games at the 1984 European Championships, a single tournament record. Cristiano Ronaldo is the all-time tournament leading goalscorer, with 14 goals in finals and a staggering 45 in qualifying matches.

UNLUCKY 13

Yugoslavian goalie Ivica Krajl had to pick the ball out of his net 13 times at Euro 2000, a tournament record in only four games. It was a bizarre tournament for Yugoslavia, who came back from 3–0 down against Slovenia, defeated the luckless Norway 1–0, and lost 4–3 to Spain with a 94th minute goal. The Netherlands then put six past them in the quarter-finals.

TOURNAMENT DREAM TEAM

Every major championship has a team of the
tournament. This is made up of the players who have
performed the best throughout. It's not always made
up of all the members of the winning team though,
usually there are players from many teams in it.
Fill in the names for the players below, and check out
the news to find out what the football pundits think –
did they make the same choices as you?

GOALKEEPER

DEFENDER

DEFENDER

DEFENDER

MIDFIELDER

MIDFIELDER

MIDFIELDER

MIDFIELDER

ATTACKER

ATTACKER

ATTACKER

THE EUROS BY NUMBERS

Cristiano Ronaldo has played the most matches in the European Championshiop finals, with 25 across 5 tournaments played. He  will be looking to extend that record this summer.

 The most championship wins are shared by Spain (1964, 2008, 2012) and Germany (1972 and 1980, as West Germany, and 1996). The Germans were also runners-up in 1976, 1992 and 2008.

Italy won the European Championship the first time they participated, in 1968. They then had to wait 53 years for a second title, when they defeated England in the final of Euro 2020.

Antonio Di Natale scored a 61st-minute goal for Italy against Spain in their opening group game of Euro 2012. It  would prove to be the last goal Spain conceded in the tournament, as they then went 509 minutes unbeaten to lift the cup.

 The veteran Hungary keeper Gábor Király is the oldest player to have appeared at the European Championships. He made his last appearance in 2016, a 4–0 defeat to Belgium in the Round of 16, at the age of 40 years and 87 days.

According to UEFA, the average live audience for the final of Euro 2020 was a whopping 328 million, across 229 territories!

FAMOUS FORMATIONS

I know it looks to some people like twenty-two players running around a pitch kicking a ball, but a vast amount of research goes into the way the teams line up and the space they occupy on a pitch. This has evolved over the years, and here are some of the significant formations that have been popular…

1 – 1 – 8

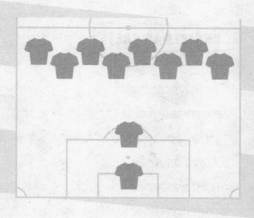

It seems almost impossible today to think that a football team would line up with one defender, one midfielder and eight forwards but this was a common formation in the 19th century and was used by England in the first ever international match against Scotland (who played a conservative 2–2–6.)

W – M

The attack was the W and the defence was the M in this seemingly complicated, hugely modern system that was popularised by the legendary Herbert Chapman at Arsenal in the 1930s. It was still popular in 1950, with a few World Cup teams playing this way, but not the way eventual winners Uruguay played. Maybe not a surprise it faded out then...

CHRISTMAS TREE

There's nothing festive about this formation! It's also known as 4–3–2–1 and it's a very defensive style, allowing solidity in the defence and not, hopefully, a gift for the opposition!

4 – 4 – 2

One of the most used – and adapted – football formations, this is still very popular in the modern game, particularly in England. In order to be successful, it requires hard work and a strong team ethic, with players covering a lot of the pitch. Some grumpy fans would say it's no wonder England haven't won a World Cup since 1966!

QUIZ TIME!

Test your knowledge of the beautiful game with this
quiz and circle the correct answers. When you've had
a go why not test your nearest and dearest too?

1 What legendary player famously called football
'the beautiful game'?
- A. Danny Blanchflower
- B. Pelé
- C. Queen Elizabeth II
- D. Vinny Jones

2 In what year was the first European Championship?
- A. 1924
- B. 1948
- C. 1960
- D. 1972

3 Which country won the first European Championship?
- A. Soviet Union
- B. France
- C. Yugoslavia
- D. Hungary

4 Albärt is the mascot of the 2022 World Cup. Which of the following was NOT an official mascot in a previous tournament?

A. Trix and Flix

B. Skillzy

C. Super Victor

D. Footix

5 When Jude Bellingham joined Real Madrid he was given the same shirt number as the legendary Zinedine Zidane. Which number?

A. 5

B. 7

C. 10

D. 11

6 Kylian Mbappé is on course to become France's all-time leading goalscorer. But who currently holds the record?

A. Michel Platini

B. Antoine Griezmann

C. Olivier Giroud

D. Thierry Henry

7 Andy Robertson's Scotland play their home games at which stadium?

A. Ibrox

C. Murrayfield

B. Tynecastle

D. Hampden Park

8 Which of the following teams has Cristiano Ronaldo NOT played for?

A. Manchester United

C. Sporting Lisbon

B. Real Madrid

D. A.C. Milan

9 Luka Modrić's Croatia side were knocked out of the 2022 World Cup in the semi finals – by which team?

A. Argentina

C. France

B. Brazil

D. Germany

10 In which year did Virgil van Dijk make his senior debut for the Netherlands?

A. 2014

C. 2016

B. 2015

D. 2017

11 Which of the following teams has never won the European Championships?

A. England

B. Italy

C. Denmark

D. Greece

12 FIFA ranks all international football teams. The number one spot is currently occupied by Argentina, but do you know which team in the 2024 European Championships ranks highest?

A. England

B. Belgium

C. France

D. Germany

13 England played the world's first international match, but in which year did they first enter the European Championships?

A. 1960

B. 1964

C. 1968

D. 1972

14 Harry Kane is England's all-time record goalscorer. Who comes second on the list?

A. Gary Lineker   C. Wayne Rooney

B. Bobby Charlton   D. Jimmy Greaves

15 There have been more than fifteen England managers since an individual took over from the International Select Committee. Which of the following was an actual England national team manager?

A. Bert Birkenstock   C. Marty Matchwinner

B. George Goalscorer   D. Walter Winterbottom

16 Which of these teams has not defeated England on penalties in a World Cup or European Championships?

A. Germany   C. Portugal

B. Spain   D. Italy

NICKNAMES

Can you match the nicknames on the left
with the teams on the right?

Les Bleus	Wales
The Magyars	England
The Red Fury	Spain
The Crescent-Stars	Hungary
Clockwork Orange	Germany
Die Mannschaft	France
The Dragons	Netherlands
The Red Devils	Belgium
The Three Lions	Turkey
The Red Crosses	Switzerland

DRIBBLE CHALLENGE

The four players below are all taking a shot on goal, but only one has the skills to hit the target and put their team a goal ahead. Follow the amazing trajectory of the ball to see which player gets the goal!

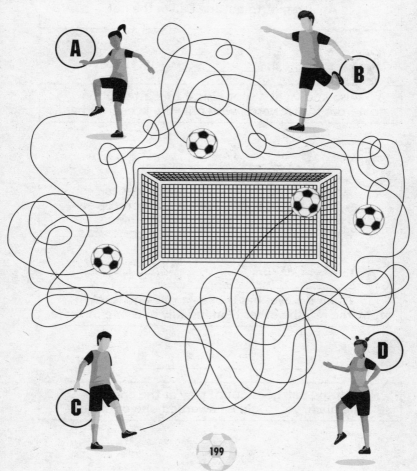

THE LANGUAGE OF FOOTBALL

1   S _ _ T

An attempt to put the ball in the net.

2   _ E _ _ _ _ Y

Also known as a spot-kick, a free attempt on goal from twelve yards, with only the keeper to beat.

3   O _ _ _ _ _ E

One of the most complicated rules to explain, this happens when a player receives a pass but is too far ahead of the game.

4   _ R _ _   K _ _ _

When a player has broken a rule and is told off by the ref, the other team usually gets one of these.

5   _ _ _ _ _ R

If the ball goes out of play at the end of the pitch, you could be awarded one of these.

Football, or soccer as some call it, comes with its own language and special terms. Can you work out the term from the definition given below?

6 _ _ _ _ _ **I N**

If the ball goes out of play on the side of the pitch, one of the teams will be awarded one of these.

7 _ **E** _ _ _ _ _

The person who is supposed to keep the match in order and keep play going...

8 _ _ _ **I** _ _ _

This is the person you expect to score the most goals.

9 _ _ **N** _ _ _ **L**

In football, scoring is great, unless it's at your end of the pitch. If you do that, it's an...

10 _ _ _ **C** _ _ _

If you are very naughty on a football pitch, you may earn yourself one of these from the person in charge.

MEMORABLE MOMENTS

The European Championships have brought joy, excitement and amazing football to the world's population for more than 60 years, and in that time, there have been some very memorable occurrences. Here we look at a few. Hopefully 2022 will have some additions to the list!

THE PANENKA, 1976

It was 2–2 after extra time in the 1976 final between Czechoslovakia and West Germany. For the first time, the tournament would be decided by penalties. Germany's Uli Hoeneß missed his kick at 4–3 to Czechoslovakia, and Antonín Panenka stepped up. Feigning to shoot with power into the corner, he simply dinked the ball delicately down the middle as the bamboozled goalie dived to his left. This kind of penalty kick is now known as 'the Panenka'.

MARCO MAGIC, 1988

The 25th of June, 1988 – the final of the European
Championships between the Netherlands and the Soviet
Union. Ruud Gullit had put the Clockwork Orange ahead
in the the 32nd minute, but the goal that would seal their
championship is one of the greatest of all time. Adri van
Tiggelen won the ball in midfield and fed Arnold Mühren
on the left wing. His high, looping cross sailed over the
entire Soviet defence and found tall, skilful striker Marco
van Basten in the far corner of the box, only a few yards
from the goal-line. Somehow, Van Basten, leaping in mid-air,
unleashed a sizzling volley from an impossible angle, arcing
perfectly over the keeper. It had to be seen to be believed.

TIKI-TAKA, 2008–2012

Spain's 'Tiki-taka' style dominated European football for
years under national team Luis Aragonés and Vicente del
Bosque, as well as club managers like Pep Guardiola. With
their short-passing, intricate, possession-based play, the
Spanish national team won the European Championships in
2008 and 2012 – plus the 2010 World Cup. Unplayable!

DANISH DELIGHT, 1992

When Yugoslavia were disqualified from Euro 1992 only
ten days before the tournament started, Denmark were
last-minute replacements, having finished as runners-up
in their qualifying group. It was a fairytale tournament
for the Danes, who defeated the reigning champions the
Netherlands in the semi-final – and then the reigning World
Cup champions Germany in the final.

GAZZA'S GOAL, 1996

After a disappointing draw in the first match of Euro 1996,
and with a difficult clash with the Netherlands coming up,
England needed a win in their second group game – against
the Auld Enemy, Scotland. England were leading 1–0
thanks to Alan Shearer when Darren Anderton's first-time
pass from the left wing found Paul Gascoigne running
into the inside left channel. As the ball dropped over his
shoulder he used his left foot to flick it over the hapless
Scottish defender Colin Hendrie, ran on into the box, and
volleyed it with his right past keeper Andy Goram. Magic!

PERFECT PLATINI, 1984

How do you follow up a hat-trick against Belgium in the
European Championship finals? France legend Michel
Platini scored another one in his very next game, against
Yugoslavia. This time it was a perfect hat-trick – left foot,
right foot, header – and in only 18 minutes, as France
recovered from a goal down to win 3–2.

ANAGRAMS

Can you work out who the players are from
these mix-ups of their names?

1. **MAYBE PLAN KIP**

2. **RADICAL ONIONS ROT**

3. **OYSTER ON BRAND**

4. **JUMBLED HEALING**

5. **NUDE BIKER ENVY**

6. **CANCEL RIDE**

7. **NOSEY EARL**

8. **CARDINAL JAVA**

9. **NO SURFER BANNED**

10. **GOODY PACK**

GERMANY 2024: WHAT TO LOOK FOR

Germany has a proud footballing tradition – the proudest, in fact, in European Championship history. It will be the third time Germany has hosted the finals, following 1998 and 2020 (when it was one of 11 different nations to host games, from Azerbaijan to Spain.)

TIMES AND DATES

Games will kick off at 3pm, 6pm and 9pm – that's 2pm, 5pm and 8pm in the UK, which is one hour behind Germany. The tournament kicks off on the 14th of June with the hosts against Scotland in Munich, and will finish with the final on the 14th of July – a mouthwatering month of football in prospect!

THE VENUES

Matches will be played at the Olympiastadion in Berlin, the BVB Stadion in Dortmund, the Arena AufSchalke in Gelsenkirchen, the Hamburg Arena, the Football Arena Munich, the Frankfurt Stadion, the Dusseldorf Arena, the Stadion Koln in Cologne, the RB Arena in Leipzig, and the Arena Stuttgart. Berlin's Olympiastadion, with over 70,000 seats, will host the final.

'LOCAL' HEROES

Two of England's stars are guaranteed a warm welcome in Germany – Jude Bellingham and Harry Kane. Kane spearheads the attack of Germany's biggest club side, Bayern Munich, while midfield maestro Jude Bellingham made his reputation at Bayern's Bundesliga rivals Borussia Dortmund.

FANS FIRST

German football is renowned for its fan-first culture. Most clubs in the Bundesliga are majority-owned by club members, there is a focus on community and youth development, and ticket prices are kept low in order to encourage supporters. The authentic passion and enthusiasm of German football fans always makes for an electric atmosphere inside the ground.

WHO'S YOUR FAVOURITE?

Ten different nations have won the European Championships, including surprise packages like Denmark and Greece – will Euro 2024 see another new name on the trophy? England are strong contenders to register their first win, but will face stiff competition from Kylian Mbappé's France, as well as former champions Germany and Spain.

ANSWERS

QUIZ TIME:

1.	B	5.	A	9.	A	13.	B
2.	C	6.	C	10.	B	14.	C
3.	A	7.	D	11.	A	15.	D
4.	D	8.	D	12.	C	16.	B

NICKNAMES:

Les Bleus	France	Die Mannschaft	Germany
Magyars	Hungary	The Dragons	Wales
The Red Fury	Spain	The Red Devils	Belgium
The Crescent-Stars	Turkey	The Three Lions	England
Clockwork Orange	Netherlands	The Red Crosses	Switzerland

DRIBBLE CHALLENGE:

Answer: Player B

THE LANGUAGE OF FOOTBALL:

1.	Shoot	5.	Corner	9.	Own Goal
2.	Penalty	6.	Throw In	10.	Red Card
3.	Offside	7.	Referee		
4.	Free Kick	8.	Striker		

ANAGRAMS:

1. Kylian Mbappé
2. Cristiano Ronaldo
3. Andy Robertson
4. Jude Bellingham
5. Kevin de Bruyne
6. Declan Rice
7. Leroy Sané
8. Dani Carvajal
9. Bruno Fernandes
10. Cody Gakpo

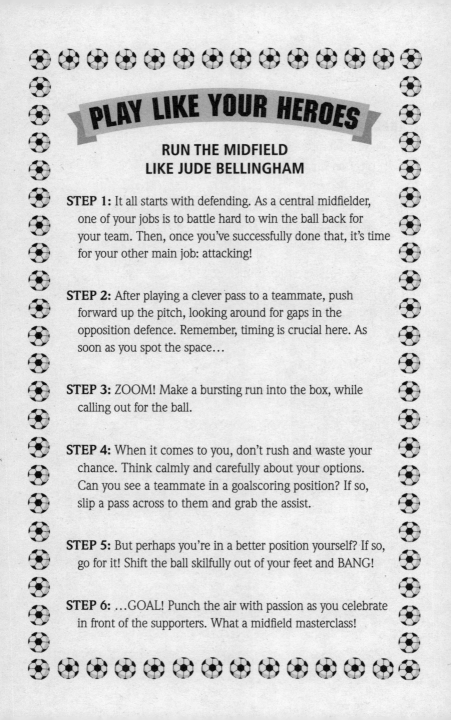

PLAY LIKE YOUR HEROES

RUN THE MIDFIELD
LIKE JUDE BELLINGHAM

STEP 1: It all starts with defending. As a central midfielder, one of your jobs is to battle hard to win the ball back for your team. Then, once you've successfully done that, it's time for your other main job: attacking!

STEP 2: After playing a clever pass to a teammate, push forward up the pitch, looking around for gaps in the opposition defence. Remember, timing is crucial here. As soon as you spot the space...

STEP 3: ZOOM! Make a bursting run into the box, while calling out for the ball.

STEP 4: When it comes to you, don't rush and waste your chance. Think calmly and carefully about your options. Can you see a teammate in a goalscoring position? If so, slip a pass across to them and grab the assist.

STEP 5: But perhaps you're in a better position yourself? If so, go for it! Shift the ball skilfully out of your feet and BANG!

STEP 6: ...GOAL! Punch the air with passion as you celebrate in front of the supporters. What a midfield masterclass!

BELLINGHAM

22 THE FACTS

NAME: Jude Bellingham

DATE OF BIRTH: 29 June 2003

PLACE OF BIRTH: Stourbridge

NATIONALITY: English

BEST FRIEND: His brother Jobe

CURRENT CLUB: Real Madrid

POSITION: Central Midfield

THE STATS

Height (cm):	186
Club appearances:	208
Club goals:	48
Club assists:	36
Club trophies:	1
International appearances:	27
International goals:	2
International trophies:	0
Ballon d'Ors:	0

★ ★ ★ **HERO RATING: 89** ★ ★ ★

PLAY LIKE YOUR HEROES

THE KYLIAN MBAPPÉ
SPRINT DRIBBLE

STEP 1: Track back to help your team in defence. It gives you more space for your sprint dribble!

STEP 2: Stay alert at all times. If an opponent plays a bad pass or your team wins the ball, you've got to be ready for the race…

STEP 3: ZOOM! Your first burst of speed is really important. Power your way past as many defenders as possible.

STEP 4: Okay, who's left? If you can beat the last defenders with pure pace, go for it!

STEP 5: If not, you'll need to use your silky skills. Stepover, stepover, stepover, ZOOM!

STEP 6: You're one-on-one with the keeper now, so you've got to stay calm. Pick your spot and shoot.

STEP 7: GOAL! It's celebration time. Run over to the fans, fold your arms across your chest and remember to look as cool as you can.

MBAPPE

7 & 10

THE FACTS

NAME: Kylian Mbappé

DATE OF BIRTH:
20 December 1998

PLACE OF BIRTH:
Bondy

NATIONALITY: French

BEST FRIEND:
Achraf Hakimi

CURRENT CLUB: PSG

POSITION: CF

THE STATS

Height (cm):	178
Club appearances:	360
Club goals:	278
Club assists:	123
Club trophies:	14
International appearances:	75
International goals:	46
International trophies:	3
Ballon d'Ors:	0

★ ★ ★ **HERO RATING: 94** ★ ★ ★

PLAY LIKE YOUR HEROES

RACE FORWARD AND CROSS
LIKE ANDY ROBERTSON

STEP 1: Warning: you're going to need lots of energy for this one! So before you get started, make sure you practise your 100m sprints.

STEP 2: When your team doesn't have the ball, stay in your position at left-back, and fight to win the ball back. But as soon as you do…

STEP 3: ZOOM! Race forward as fast as you can up the left wing, calling for the ball.

STEP 4: When it arrives, take a touch to control the ball and a second to look up and see where your teammates are in the box. Then…

STEP 5: WHIP! Curl the ball around the defenders and into the danger area, with plenty of power and loads of accuracy.

STEP 6: BANG!... GOAL! As your striker rushes towards the fans, race over to celebrate with them. You deserve to get at least some of the glory after your amazing assist.

ROBERTSON

26 THE FACTS

NAME: Andrew Robertson

DATE OF BIRTH: 11 March 1994

PLACE OF BIRTH: Glasgow

NATIONALITY: Scottish

BEST FRIEND: James Milner

CURRENT CLUB: Liverpool

POSITION: Left Back

THE STATS

Height (cm):	178
Club appearances:	487
Club goals:	21
Club assists:	83
Club trophies:	8
International appearances:	62
International goals:	3
International trophies:	0
Ballon d'Ors:	0

★ ★ ★ **HERO RATING: 86** ★ ★ ★

PLAY LIKE YOUR HEROES

THE CRISTIANO RONALDO GOAL CELEBRATION

STEP 1: Score an amazing goal.

STEP 2: Run towards the fans, smiling, nodding and pointing at yourself.

STEP 3: As you get towards the corner flag, jump into the air with your arms up high.

STEP 4: In mid-air, spin around so that you now have your back to the fans and they can all see the name and number on the back of your shirt.

STEP 5: As you land, keep your feet wide apart and bring your arms down dramatically until they are slightly behind your body.

STEP 6: Scream loudly with your mouth wide open in an 'O' shape.

STEP 7: Hold that pose until all of your team-mates run over and hug you.

RONALDO

7

THE FACTS

NAME:
Cristiano Ronaldo

DATE OF BIRTH:
5 February 1985

PLACE OF BIRTH:
Funchal, Madeira

NATIONALITY: Portugal

BEST FRIEND: Nani

CURRENT CLUB: Al Nassr

POSITION: CF

THE STATS

Height (cm):	187
Club appearances:	1,000
Club goals:	744
Club trophies:	34
International appearances:	205
International goals:	128
International trophies:	2
Ballon d'Ors:	5

★ ★ ★ **HERO RATING: 91** ★ ★ ★

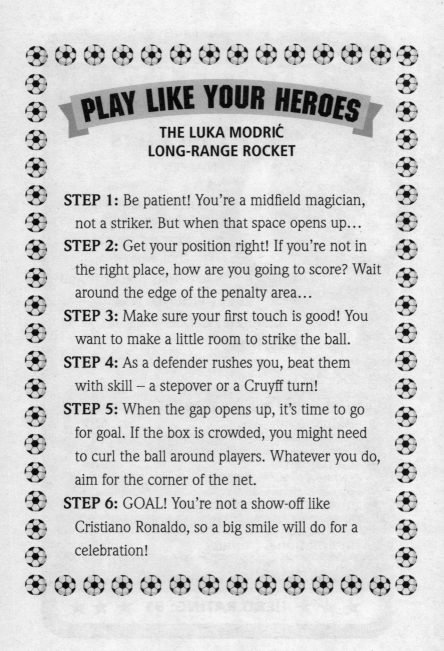

PLAY LIKE YOUR HEROES

THE LUKA MODRIĆ
LONG-RANGE ROCKET

STEP 1: Be patient! You're a midfield magician, not a striker. But when that space opens up…

STEP 2: Get your position right! If you're not in the right place, how are you going to score? Wait around the edge of the penalty area…

STEP 3: Make sure your first touch is good! You want to make a little room to strike the ball.

STEP 4: As a defender rushes you, beat them with skill – a stepover or a Cruyff turn!

STEP 5: When the gap opens up, it's time to go for goal. If the box is crowded, you might need to curl the ball around players. Whatever you do, aim for the corner of the net.

STEP 6: GOAL! You're not a show-off like Cristiano Ronaldo, so a big smile will do for a celebration!

MODRIC

10 **THE FACTS**

NAME: LUKA MODRIĆ

DATE OF BIRTH:
9 September 1985

PLACE OF BIRTH:
Zadar

NATIONALITY:
Croatian

BEST FRIEND:
Vedran Ćorluka

CURRENT CLUB: Real Madrid

POSITION: CM

THE STATS

Height (cm):	172
Club appearances:	774
Club goals:	85
Club assists:	129
Club trophies:	27
International appearances:	172
International goals:	24
International trophies:	0
Ballon d'Ors:	1

★ ★ ★ **HERO RATING: 88** ★ ★ ★

PLAY LIKE YOUR HEROES

VIRGIL VAN DIJK'S DEADLY DEFENDING

STEP 1: Keep talking and organising your teammates, from the first kick until the final whistle.

STEP 2: Deal with any attacks as calmly as possible. You want to make defending look like a casual walk in the park.

STEP 3: Don't rush in and make a clumsy tackle. Watch carefully and wait patiently. Be smart and make the striker make the next move.

STEP 4: Slow striker? Use your super-speed to outsprint him.

STEP 5: Small striker? Use your super-strength to outmuscle him.

STEP 6: If all else fails, stretch out your long leg at the last, crucial second, and clear the ball out for a corner.

STEP 7: Right, back to the talking. Clap and shout and wave angrily at your teammates: 'Where were you?' 'Get back!'

VAN DIJK

4 THE FACTS

NAME: Virgil van Dijk

DATE OF BIRTH: 8 July 1991

PLACE OF BIRTH: Breda

NATIONALITY: Dutch

BEST FRIEND: Gini Wijnaldum

CURRENT CLUB: Liverpool

POSITION: CB

THE STATS

Height (cm):	193
Club appearances:	521
Club goals:	53
Club assists:	26
Club trophies:	10
International appearances:	64
International goals:	7
International trophies:	0
Ballon d'Ors:	0

★ ★ ★ **HERO RATING: 90** ★ ★ ★

CAN'T GET ENOUGH OF
ULTIMATE FOOTBALL HEROES?

**Check out heroesfootball.com
for quizzes, games, and competitions!**

**Plus join the Ultimate Football Heroes
Fan Club to score exclusive content
and be the first to hear about
new books and events.
heroesfootball.com/subscribe/**